This book is a gift to:

_____

From:

_____

Date:

_____

Meet Me in the Meadow

© 2010 Christian Art Gifts, RSA
Christian Art Gifts Inc., IL, USA

© 2010 Roy Lessin

Designed by Christian Art Gifts

Images used under license from Shutterstock.com

Unless otherwise indicated, all Scripture quotations are taken from the *Holy Bible*,
New King James Version. Copyright © 1979, 1980, 1982 by Thomas Nelson
Publishers, Inc. Used by permission. All rights reserved.

Scripture quotations marked NIV are taken from the *Holy Bible*, New International Version®
NIV®. Copyright © 1973, 1978, 1984 by International Bible Society.
Used by permission of Zondervan Publishing House. All rights reserved.

Scripture quotations marked NLT are taken from the *Holy Bible*, New Living Translation, first
edition, copyright © 1996. Used by permission of Tyndale House Publishers, Inc., Carol Stream,
Illinois 60188. All rights reserved.

Scripture quotations marked AMP are taken from The Amplified® Bible.
Old Testament copyright © 1965, 1987 by Zondervan Corporation.
New Testament copyright © 1958, 1987 by The Lockman Foundation. Used by permission.

Scripture quotations are taken from the *Holy Bible*, King James Version.
Copyright © 1962 by The Zondervan Corporation. Used by permission.

Scripture references are taken from the New American Standard Bible (NASB),
© 1960, 1962, 1963, 1968, 1971, 1972, 1973, 1975, 1977 by the Lockman
Foundation. All rights reserved. Used by permission.

Printed in China

ISBN 978-1-77036-547-6

11 12 13 14 15 16 17 18 19 20 – 11 10 9 8 7 6 5 4 3 2

MEET ME
in the
MEADOW

Roy Lessin

christian
art gifts ®

January

Into His Meadow

*Until the Spirit is poured upon us from on high,
and the wilderness becomes a fruitful field, and the
fruitful field is counted as a forest. Then justice
will dwell in the wilderness, and righteousness
remain in the fruitful field. The work of
righteousness will be peace, and the effect of
righteousness, quietness and assurance forever.
My people will dwell in a peaceful habitation,
in secure dwellings, and in quiet resting places.*
– Isaiah 32:15-18 –

"Menuchah" is a Hebrew word that means *peacefully,
stillness,* or the *quiet resting place.* In your walk with
Jesus day by day, "menuchah" can be understood as
an invitation to follow the Lord, your Good Shepherd,
into His meadow – His dwelling place, His quiet place,
His resting place, His protected place, His safe place,
His nurturing place. This is where your heart will be
comforted, your love deepened, your faith strengthened,
and your soul renewed.

Once

You, who were once far from God, have now been drawn close to His heart (Eph. 2:13).

You, who were once in spiritual poverty, have now been made lavishly rich (Eph. 2:7).

You, who were once without fruit, have now been made to flourish (John 15:16).

You, who were once extremely needy, have now been made complete (Col. 2:10).

You, who were once alone and empty, have now been immersed in love (Eph. 3:18-19).

You, who were once a wandering sheep, have now been brought into the fold (1 Peter 2:25).

You, who were once an alien, have now been made a citizen of heaven (Eph. 2:19).

You, who were once an orphan, have now been adopted into God's family (Rom. 8:15).

Leave Jesus?

*From that time many of His disciples went
back and walked with Him no more. Then Jesus
said to the twelve, "Do you also want to go away?"
But Simon Peter answered Him, "Lord, to whom
shall we go? You have the words of eternal life."*
– John 6:67-68 –

Leave Jesus? Where else could we go?
We could never have a richer life;
We could never find a better way;
We could never know a deeper love;
We could never see a greater glory;
We could never belong to a surer Kingdom;
We could never possess a nobler purpose;
We could never stand upon a firmer foundation;
We could never receive a fuller joy;
We could never hear a higher call;
We could never walk with a truer friend.

Being Used by God to Bless Others

*"Master, we have toiled all the night
and have taken nothing."*
– Luke 5:5 –

What was the reason for this? They understood the work. Had they gone about the toil unskillfully? No. Had they lacked industry? No. They had toiled. Had they lacked perseverance? No. They had toiled all the night. Was there a deficiency of fish in the sea? Certainly not, for as soon as the Master came, they swam to the net in schools. What, then, is the reason? It is because there is no power in themselves apart from the presence of Jesus! Without Christ we can do nothing, but with Him we can do all things. Christ's presence confers success.

– CHARLES H. SPURGEON

I used to ask God if He would come and help me. Then I asked God if I might come and help Him; then I ended by asking God to do His own work through me.

– HUDSON TAYLOR

Men ask for a rainbow in the cloud; but I would ask more from Thee. I would be, in my cloud, myself a rainbow – a minister to others' joy.

– GEORGE MATHESON

Inspected

*Search me, O God, and know my heart: try me,
and know my anxieties: and see if there be any wicked
way in me, and lead me in the way everlasting.*
– Psalm 139:23-24 –

I find it extremely comforting and reassuring to have my wife take a good look at me before I head out the front door to start the day. I know that if she sees something I have missed in my appearance she will let me know. If she sees dirt on my face, a stain on my shirt, a belt loop missed, or a color combination that is not working, she will simply, clearly, and lovingly let me know about it. Her caring sense of observation has saved me much embarrassment through the years.

It's also equally comforting and reassuring to let the Holy Spirit give us "the once over" before we head out the door to start the day. How wise we would be to daily let Him inspect us to be sure everything is in order – to be sure there is not resentment or bitterness hardening our hearts, to be sure there is no anxiety or worry weighing on our thoughts, and to be sure there is no unbelief or doubts clouding our spirits. How blessed our day would be if we could leave the house each morning knowing it is well with our souls.

Blessings

*"The L*ORD *bless you and keep you;*
*the L*ORD *make His face shine upon you,*
*and be gracious to you; the L*ORD *lift up*
His countenance upon you, and give you peace."
– Numbers 6:24-26 –

F. W. Boreham tells the true account of an elderly Scottish woman who, just before she died, lifted her feeble, thin hand and gently placed it upon his head as he was kneeling in prayer at her bedside. With a thick Scottish accent she pronounced this benediction over him:

The Lord bless ye, the Lord bless ye and keep ye! The Lord bless ye in your youth and in your auld age! The Lord bless ye in your basket and in your store! The Lord bless ye in your kirk and in your hame! The Lord bless ye in your guid wife and in your wee bairns! The Lord bless ye in your gaeings out and in your comings in frae this time forth and even for evermair!

And so may the Lord bless you!

Fear and Faith

Look, the LORD your God has set the land before you;
go up and possess it, as the LORD God of your fathers
has spoken to you; do not fear or be discouraged.
– Deuteronomy 1:21 –

Fear is a thief;
    faith is a rewarder.
Fear questions and retreats;
    faith takes things God has promised and goes forward.
Fear lets the inheritance we have in Christ go unclaimed;
    faith takes hold of its possessions.
Fear quivers;
    faith fights.
Fear says, "later";
    faith says, "now."
Fear is defeat;
    faith is victory.
Fear says "You will be overcome";
    faith says, "You are an overcomer."
Fear tears you down;
    faith raises you up.
Fear says, "how?";
    faith says, "God!"

Holiness and Glory (I)

"Holy, holy, holy is the LORD of hosts;
the whole earth is full of His glory!"
– Isaiah 6:3 –

Most often, when people in the Bible encountered God they either trembled, fell on their face, worshiped, or took the shoes from off their feet because they were standing on holy ground. Like Isaiah, we need to see the Lord "high and lifted up."

It is the Lord's glory and holiness (His majesty) that brings the fear of the Lord to our hearts.

It is His glory and holiness that keeps us from an unholy familiarity toward God; it is His glory and holiness that keeps us from cavalier attitudes and actions toward the things of God; It is the glory and holiness of God that keeps us from becoming careless in our walk, careless in our speech, careless in our humor, and careless in our relationship toward God.

Holiness and Glory (II)

God's holiness and glory are linked together.

> God's glory should silence us,
> God's holiness should humble us;
> God's glory should lift us up,
> God's holiness should clean us up;
> God's glory should adorn us,
> God's holiness should transform us;
> God's glory should excite us,
> God's holiness should ignite us.

It has been said that scientists look into space and study, while believers look into space and worship. Do your eyes see Him? Does your heart adore Him? Do you cry out "Holy, holy, holy ... the whole earth is filled with His glory?"

"Earth's crammed with heaven,
And every common bush afire with God,
But only he who sees takes off his shoes."

– ELIZABETH BARRETT BROWNING

God Is, Was, and Always Will Be

Everything that God is today He has always been; everything that He has always been He will always be. Yesterday, God was there. Today, God is here. Tomorrow, God will be there.

Was He your peace yesterday?
He will be your peace today.
Is He your peace today?
He will be your peace tomorrow.

Was He your provider yesterday?
He will be your provider today.
Is He your provider today?
He will be your provider tomorrow.

O God, renew us in Thy love today,
For our tomorrow we have not a care,
Who blessed our yesterday
Will meet us there.

– AMY CARMICHAEL

Heaven Is Better

Eye has not seen, nor ear heard, nor have
entered into the heart of man the things
which God has prepared for those who love Him.
– 1 Corinthians 2:9 –

It is good to walk the path of a pilgrim;
    It is better to arrive at your glorious destination.
It is good to live the life of faith;
    It is better to receive faith's final reward.
It is good to overcome and persevere;
    It is better to wear the victor's crown.
It is good to live for Jesus day by day;
    It is better to see Jesus face to face.

Quiet Hearts in Troubled Times

*"Let not your heart be troubled; you
believe in God, believe also in Me."*
– John 14:1 –

**God wants us to have quiet hearts, not troubled
thoughts.**

We should never know the music of the harp if the strings
were left untouched nor enjoy the juice of the grape if it were
not trodden in the wine-press. We would never discover
the sweet perfume of cinnamon if it were not pressed and
beaten or feel the warmth of fire if the coals were not utterly
consumed. The wisdom and power of the great Workman are
discovered by the trials through which His vessels of mercy are
permitted to pass.

– CHARLES H. SPURGEON

Truth

God is Truth
But the Lord is the true God and the God of truth (the God Who is Truth). He is the living God and the everlasting King (Jer. 10:10 AMP).

Jesus is the Truth
Jesus said to him, I am the Way and the Truth and the Life; no one comes to the Father except by (through) Me (John 14:6 AMP).

The Holy Spirit is the Spirit of Truth
The Spirit of Truth, Whom the world cannot receive (welcome, take to its heart), because it does not see Him or know and recognize Him. But you know and recognize Him, for He lives with you [constantly] and will be in you (John 14:17 AMP).

The Word of God is Truth
Sanctify them [purify, consecrate, separate them for Yourself, make them holy] by the Truth; Your Word is Truth (John 17:17 AMP).

Our Relationship to Truth

We should –

- Know the Truth (John 8:32).
- Practice Truth (John 3:21).
- Worship in Truth (John 4:23).
- Bear witness to the Truth (John 5:33).
- Speak the Truth (John 8:46).
- Be guided by the Truth (John 16:13).
- Be sanctified by the Truth (John 17:17).
- Be of the Truth (John 18:37).
- Obey the Truth (Rom. 2:8).
- Rejoice in the Truth (1 Cor. 13:6).
- Do nothing against the Truth (2 Cor. 13:8).
- Be girded with the Truth (Eph. 6:14).
- Love the Truth (2 Thess. 2:10).
- Believe the Truth (2 Thess. 2:12).
- Rightly handle and skillfully teach the Truth (2 Tim. 2:15).
- Welcome the Truth (2 Tim. 3:8).
- Listen to the Truth (2 Tim. 4:4).
- Be established in Truth (2 Peter 1:12).
- Walk in Truth (2 John 1:4).

For His Glory

For this reason we also, since the day we heard it,
do not cease to pray for you, and to ask that you may be
filled with the knowledge of His will in all wisdom and
spiritual understanding; that you may walk worthy
of the Lord, fully pleasing Him, being fruitful in every
good work and increasing in the knowledge of God.
– Colossians 1:9-10 –

Each step is a right step
   when it follows His pathway.
Each word is a loving word
   when it comes from His heart.
Each touch is a healing touch
   when it is motivated by His compassion.
Each decision is a wise decision
   when it is made according to His will.
Each work is a good work
   when it is done for His glory.

Our True Guide

If I were going on a safari, I would want a guide who had the fire power to stop a charging wild beast from devouring me. If I were traveling through the desert, I would want a guide who knew where all the wells were located. If I were traveling through the jungle, I would want a guide who knew the trail and could get me to my destination.

As we travel through life we don't need tips or well intended advice, we need a true Guide. We need a true Guide because we need to be guided. Sadly, many people seek guidance from guides who do not know the way and lead us to dead ends. God is the only true, trustworthy, fully qualified Guide there is who can rightly direct our steps and lead us in the way we should go. If we have the right Guide, we will know the right guidance.

Knowing God's Guidance

We must first yield ourselves to God before we can know His guidance. God wants to rule in our hearts before He guides us and directs our steps. Guidance comes out of relationship. Elisabeth Elliot, in her book on guidance, reminds us that "When God spoke to Moses from out of the burning bush, first came the 'I Am' then came the 'Do this.'" When it comes to our future, Elisabeth Elliot also reminds us that, "God knows the way, He has been over every foot of it."

The psalmist David tells us in Psalm 31:3, "For You are my rock and my fortress; therefore, for Your name's sake, lead me and guide me." Before David asked God to lead and guide him, David knew that God was his rock and fortress – his safety, his protection, and security.

Because David trusted God for his life, he could also trust God for his future. For David, God's guidance also meant God's glory. David did not ask God to guide him in ways that would make David look good, but that would exalt the Lord's name.

God's Guidance Settled in our Heart

For the believer, God's guidance is one of the greatest issues that must be settled in the heart. God's guidance is what separates the believer from the world.

God is looking for those who want His way in their lives instead of their own way; His mind instead of their point of view; His wisdom instead of their strategy; His timing instead of their schedules; His steps instead of their shortcuts.

The one who knows God's guidance is the one who has said in his heart, "God, I am trusting in your plans for my life instead of pursuing my own plans."

As Your Guide God Will ...

- Tell you when it's time to go (Gen. 12:1).
- Guide you in His strength (Exod. 15:13).
- Give you rest (Exod. 33:14).
- Go before you (Num. 14:14).
- Light your darkness (2 Sam. 22:29).
- Provide for you (Neh. 9:20).
- Lead you in paths of righteousness (Ps. 23:3).
- Guide you in truth and faithfulness (Ps. 25:5).
- Teach you His way (Ps. 25:9).
- Keep His eye upon you (Ps. 32:8).
- Give you His counsel (Ps. 73:24).
- Correct your course if you start to drift (Isa. 30:21).
- Not leave you or forsake you (Isa. 42:16).
- Nurture you (Isa. 58:11).
- Be your companion (Jer. 3:4).

Seeing God in our Trials

Never complain of your birth, your training, your employments, your hardships; never to fancy that you could be something if only you had a different lot and sphere assigned you. God understands His own plan, and He knows what you want a great deal better than you do. The very things that you most deprecate, as fatal limitations or obstructions, are probably what you most want. What you call hindrances, obstacles, discouragements, are probably God's opportunities.

– H. BUSHNELL

Have we not seen Thy shining garment's hem
Floating at dawn across the golden skies,
Through thin blue veils at noon, bright majesties,
Seen starry hosts delight to gem
The splendor that shall be Thy diadem?

– AMY CARMICHAEL

Theology

Theology is a good word and a vitally important one. It means the study of God, especially His attributes and character. Any study of God must be based upon the Bible, for it is here and here alone that God has given us a written revelation of Himself. Sound, biblical theology is essential for your Christian life, for right thinking about God, and for you to be able to walk with Him in truth.

Today, there is a great deal of confusion about who God is. We need to be wise and discerning. The truth of Scripture must form our theology and not the opinions of man. There are voices today that are telling us about a God they have created out of their own imagination. Some, in an attempt to make God relevant to our culture, have tried to pull Him down to our level of thinking and living.

We need to see the Lord in clarity, in reality, and in truth. We need to see Him and worship Him in spirit and in truth. As we do, instead of having a theology that pulls God down, He will have one that truly lifts Him up.

Who Is Interested in You?

"Yes, I have loved you with an everlasting love; therefore with lovingkindness I have drawn you."
– Jeremiah 31:3 –

Business is interested in you as a consumer.

Banks are interested in you as an investor.

Politicians are interested in you as a voter.

Researchers are interested in you as a statistic.

Sports teams are interested in you as a fan.

Doctors are interested in you as a patient.

Lawyers are interested in you as a client.

Stores are interested in you as a shopper.

Organizations are interested in you as a member.

But God is interested in you as a person, made in His image, His precious child whom He loves.

God's Best to You

God can only give the best to you, because second best is not a part of His nature, His character, or His heart. If you cast yourself upon Him, He will not let you slip through His hands; if you drink from His fountain, you will never taste of tainted waters; if you eat at His table, you will never find stale bread; if you walk in His footsteps, you will never be led into pathways of confusion.

Man finds it hard to get what he wants, because he does not want the best. God finds it hard to give, because He would give the best, and man will not take it.

– GEORGE MACDONALD

Our Savior from Sin

God sent His Son into the world to die upon a cross. He didn't die as a martyr, but as our Savior. He didn't die for a noble cause, but for our sins. Jesus Christ died to save us from every stain of sin, every shame of sin, and every pain of sin.

When Jesus shed His blood for our sins, God's justice was satisfied. The blood of Jesus Christ stands as the only redemptive price God will accept for the cleansing and forgiveness of our sins. Because of the blood of Jesus, God says to us, "Turn to Me and I will cleanse you. I will wash you. I will forgive you."

Because of the shed blood of Jesus Christ, God says to you, "Come now, and let us reason together," says the Lord, "Though your sins are like scarlet, they shall be as white as snow; though they are red like crimson, they shall be as wool" (Isa. 1:18).

Beautiful Savior

Have your sins weighed you down?
    Let Jesus lift you up.
Have your sins broken your heart?
    Let Jesus heal you.
Have your sins had you bound?
    Let Jesus free you.
Have your sins condemned you?
    Let Jesus speak His words of forgiveness over your life.

Let Him embrace you in His arms of grace; let Him cover you with His mercy; let Him draw you close to His heart.
    As you receive His forgiveness, hear Him say to you ...

For as the heaven is high above the earth,
so great is His mercy toward them that fear Him.
As far as the east is from the west, so far hath
He removed our transgressions from us.
– Psalm 103:11-12 (KJV) –

It Is Written

David ... served his own generation by the will of God.
– Acts 13:36 –

Life was never intended to be a gamble. "Chance" does not rule our universe; "luck" does not influence your existence; "fate" does not guide your destiny.

An advertisement on a highway displayed a picture of a cute baby. Next to the picture was the statement, "If they only came with instructions." The billboard was clever, but it was also a sad reminder that many people believe it is up to us to figure out the meaning and purpose of our lives. Thankfully, through His Word, God has provided written instructions for each life that comes into the world.

God did not bring you into this world to live without a purpose, to exist without a reason, or function without meaning. You are not here because of chance. You are a unique creation of God. He loves you, and cares about you. God desires to use you, according to His will, to make Him known to this generation.

Jesus Loves You

That Christ may dwell in your hearts through faith;
that you, being rooted and grounded in love,
may be able to comprehend with all the saints what
is the width and length and depth and height – to
know the love of Christ which passes knowledge;
that you may be filled with all the fullness of God.
– Ephesians 3:17-19 –

Jesus loves you,
    no one could be kinder;
He cares for you,
    no one could be more thoughtful;
He prays for you,
    no one could be more understanding;
He guides you,
    no one could more watchful;
He keeps you,
    no one could be more protective;
He blesses you,
    no one could more generous.

God's Power Works Wonders

Now to Him who is able to do exceedingly abundantly above all that we ask or think, according to the power that works in us, to Him be the glory.
– Ephesians 3:20 –

God is ALL-powerful. When we hear about God's power we often think about wonders and miracles. These can draw large crowds, cause people to travel long distances, and stir up great excitement. The Bible gives us many glimpses into God's wonder-working power – healing a sick body (Mark 1:30-31), turning water into wine (John 2:9), feeding a multitude (Matt. 14:19), calming a stormy sea (Matt. 8:27), and raising the dead (John 11:43).

Wonders and miracles are manifestations of God's power that glorify Him, but they are not the only way God's power is revealed to us. In Ephesians 3:20 Paul tells about the power of God that works within us. Here, the emphasis is not upon what God's power can do *for* us, but what God's power can do *to* us. Sadly, the subject of miracles typically draws more attention than the subject of sanctification. There are many who will seek God for a new manifestation, but will not seek Him for a new disposition; for a new sign, but not for a new heart; for a new wonder, but not for a new life.

God's Power Changes Us

In Colossians 1:10-12 we discover that God's power can change us from within:

> That you may walk worthy of the Lord, fully pleasing Him, being fruitful in every good work and increasing in the knowledge of God; strengthened with all might, according to His glorious power, for all patience and longsuffering with joy; giving thanks to the Father who has qualified us to be partakers of the inheritance of the saints in the light.

It takes the power of God to cause a crippled man to walk, to open the eyes of someone who cannot see, to bring hearing to deaf ears, and to set someone free from demonic powers. But, it also takes the power of God to stop someone from grumbling and complaining, from being impatient, from giving up, from being ungrateful, or from being controlled by wrong attitudes.

We experience the power of God to change us when we are cleansed by the blood of Jesus Christ, when we take up our cross and embrace His will, when we are filled and controlled by the Holy Spirit, when we walk in obedience to His Word, and when we trust Him with all our hearts.

God's Power Is Available to Us

People can be *touched* by the power of God without being *changed* by the power of God (the account of the healing of the ten lepers in Luke 17:12-19 illustrates this). As wonderful as it is to experience God's supernatural power through wonders and miracles, we must also trust in God's transforming power to live meaningful, victorious lives.

It takes God's power to remain on a task when you know it is not time to move on; to get the job done when you don't feel like it; to be faithful when other things want to pull you away; to do what's right when no one is watching; to rejoice when you would rather mope; to keep gratitude in your heart when you would rather complain; to continue on in hope when things around you are dark.

Each of us needs God's power to live a godly life, and thankfully, that power is available to us. Second Peter 1:3 tells us, "According as His divine power hath given unto us all things that pertain unto life and godliness, through the knowledge of Him that hath called us to glory and virtue."

God's Care for You

Your sigh is able to move the heart of Jehovah. Your whisper can incline His ear to you. Your prayer can stay His hand, and your faith can move His arm. Do not think that God sits on high taking no account of you.

– CHARLES H. SPURGEON

For the eyes of the LORD run to and fro throughout the whole earth, to show Himself strong on behalf of those whose heart is loyal to Him.

– 2 CHRONICLES 16:9

It is not the multitude of hard duties, it is not constraint and contention that advance us in our Christian course. On the contrary, it is the yielding of our wills without restriction and without choice, to tread cheerfully every day in the path in which Providence leads us, to seek nothing, to be discouraged by nothing, to see our duty in the present moment, to trust all else without reserve to the will and power of God.

– FRANÇOIS FENÉLON

February

New Day

*Then, as soon as they had come to land, they
saw a fire of coals there, and fish laid on it, and bread.
Jesus said to them, "Bring some of the fish which you
have just caught" ... "Come and eat breakfast."*
– John 21:9,12 –

Jesus gathered those He loved around an open fire in the
early morning hours to share some breakfast together.
He used this informal setting to reveal Himself to them
after His resurrection. He reassured them in their uncertainty, and refreshed them in their weariness. He
turned a difficult evening into a glorious new day.

What will this day be for you? Let Jesus' words define
it; let Jesus' will direct it; let Jesus' love decide it.

Being Still

In his book *Emblems of the Holy Spirit*, Frederick E. Marsh shares the following thoughts. Let your heart rest in the stillness and the quiet place your faith finds in Christ alone.

In every life
There's a pause that is better than onward rush,
Better than hewing, or mightiest doing;
'Tis the standing still at sovereign will.
There's a hush that is better than ardent speech,
Better than sighing, or wilderness crying;
'Tis the being still at sovereign will.
The pause and the hush sing a double song
In unison low, and for all time long.
O, human soul. God's working plan
Goes on, nor needs the aid of man,
Stand still, and see,
Be still, and know.

The God of Hope

Who takes our hands within the fight,
And makes us triumph by His might?
The God of hope.

Who lifts us up on eagle's wings,
And gives our hearts a song to sing?
The God of hope.

Who brings us to His loving side,
And keeps us close as we abide?
The God of hope.

Who moves our feet to higher ground,
And takes us where His grace is found?
The God of hope.

Who floods our eyes with heaven's light,
And rescues us from darkest night?
The God of hope.

Who comes to us in perfect love,
And turns our hearts to things above?
The God of hope.

There's Something Different About You

But you are a chosen generation, a royal priesthood,
a holy nation, His own special people, that you
may proclaim the praises of Him who called you
out of darkness into His marvelous light.
– 1 Peter 2:9 –

There's something different about you:

- In uncertain times you are secure;
- While others walk in fear, you walk by faith;
- In a world that is like sand, your feet stand upon a rock;
- With worry all around you, you have peace beyond understanding;
- In the midst of heaviness and discouragement, you have joy unspeakable;
- In troubled times, you have every comfort and consolation;
- While the world wonders what will happen next, you have hope strongly planted in your heart.

There's Something Different About You

May you be blessed by the LORD,
Who made heaven and earth.
– Psalm 115:15 –

There's something about you:

- Your heart has been toward the Lord, and His heart has been toward you;
- You have taken care of the things that concern Him, and He has taken care of the things that concern you;
- You have given Him all that is yours, and He has given you all that is His;
- You have waited upon Him, and He will not disappoint you;
- Your plans are now His purposes; your commitments are based on His leading;
- Your desires fit into His design;
- You have sought for His highest and He has given you His best.

Contentment in Jesus (I)

I want them to have complete confidence
that they understand God's mysterious plan,
which is Christ himself. In him lie hidden
all the treasures of wisdom and knowledge.
– Colossians 2:2-3 NLT –

His water quenches your thirst;
    you don't need to dig other cisterns.
His bread fills your hunger;
    you don't need to gather up crumbs.
His banqueting table is extravagant;
    you don't need to eat at outside diners.
His presence is fullness of joy;
    you don't need to seek ways to find fulfillment.
His peace passes understanding;
    you don't need to get an artificial fix.
His will is perfect;
    you don't need to acquire a better plan.
His wisdom is flawless;
    you don't need to listen to the world's point of view.

Contentment in Jesus (2)

*So he is first in everything. For God in all his
fullness was pleased to live in Christ, and through
him God reconciled everything to himself.*
– *Colossians 1:18-20* NLT –

His grace is sufficient;
    you don't need to obtain superficial help.
His redemption is complete;
    you don't need to hunt for another savior.
His covenant is certain;
    you don't need to read a different guarantee.
His provision meets my needs;
    you don't need to be on a quest for more.
His kingdom is unshakable;
    you don't need to find a more secure place to stand.
His smile is enough;
    you don't need to seek the applause of others.
His life is glorious;
    you don't need to look for another reason to live.
His return is sure;
    you don't need to let my heart be troubled.

God's Love Expressed through Us

Beloved, let us love one another, for love is of God;
and everyone who loves is born of God and knows God.
He who does not love does not know God, for God is love.
In this the love of God was manifested toward us,
that God has sent His only begotten Son into the world,
that we might live through Him. In this is love,
not that we loved God, but that He loved us and sent
His Son to be the propitiation for our sins. Beloved,
if God so loved us, we also ought to love one another.
– 1 John 4:7-11 –

Every attribute of God is an attribute of love.

Every expression of God is an expression of love.

Every word of God is a word of love.

Every gift of God is a gift of love.

Every motivation of God is a motivation of love.

Every choice of God is a choice of love.

Every response of God is a response of love.

The Attributes of Love (I)

And we have known and believed the love that
God has for us. God is love, and he who abides
in love abides in God, and God in him.
– 1 John 4:16 –

Righteousness is the character of love;
   Holiness is the beauty of love;
Omnipotence is the power of love;
   Omnipresence is the nearness of love;
Omniscience is the mind of love;
   Judgment is the protection of love;
Grace is the favor of love.

The Attributes of Love (II)

We love Him because He first loved us.
– 1 John 4:19 –

Goodness is the practice of love;
    Kindness is the attitude of love;
Care is the tenderness of love;
    Majesty is the glory of love;
Giving is the expression of love;
    Peace is the rest of love;
Joy is the celebration of love.

Zero Tolerance

Be anxious for nothing, but in everything
by prayer and supplication, with thanksgiving,
let your requests be made known to God; and the
peace of God, which surpasses all understanding, will
guard your hearts and minds through Christ Jesus.
– Philippians 4:6-7 –

How much anxiety should you carry in your heart?
　　How much worry should fill your mind?
How much fear should agitate your soul?

The best and only policy toward anxiety, worry, and fear is "zero tolerance". Through prayer, you must close the door to every enemy of God's peace. It is His peace within you that will stand guard against the things that want to trouble you and give you unrest.

Your Work Matters (I)

Whatever you do, do it heartily, as to the Lord and not to men, knowing that from the Lord you will receive the reward of the inheritance; for you serve the Lord Christ.
– Colossians 3:23-24 –

This Scripture is packed with significance regarding your work:

"Whatever you do ... "
From God's point of view, whatever it is that you are doing is significant. God does not want any of us to struggle with insignificance. Your name may appear at the bottom of a work flow chart, or you may be at the low end of the pay scale, but that has nothing to do with significance. What you do, however big or small, is an assignment from the Lord and that makes it significant.

"Do it heartily ... "
The attitude in which you do your work is important to God. God is saying, "Put your heart into the work I've given you to do." God wants you to approach your work whole-heartedly, with thankfulness and not complaint. Having the right attitude can make all the difference in your day.

Your Work Matters (II)

"As to the Lord and not to men ... "
There is a huge trap that awaits you when you do your work to please people instead of God. When people don't give you the recognition you are seeking, you can easily get discouraged with your work. Trying to please people can also create striving within you and rob you of your joy. God's way to freedom and joy is for you to do your work as unto Him.

"From the Lord you will receive the reward ... "
Getting a pay check is a great reward for your work, but the reward you will receive from the Lord is far greater. Pay checks will help you with your temporal needs, but your eternal rewards will far outshine and outlast them all.

"For you serve the Lord Christ ... "
You work at a business but you don't work for a business. You work for the Lord. He is your real boss. Your highest purpose at work each day is to please Him, to bring a smile to His face, and to have Him say over your life "I am well pleased." At the end of the day, that is what really matters.

The "Perfect Peace" Ratio

Do not fret ... it only causes harm.
– Psalm 37:8 –

How much peace does it take to balance fretting in our lives? The answer is that there is no "balancing point" for fret. We cannot balance something in our lives that is not to be there. God wants the peace/fret ratio in our lives to be as follows:

Peace 100%
Fretting 0%

His Kingdom within You (I)

*The kingdom of God is not eating and drinking, but
righteousness and peace and joy in the Holy Spirit.*
– Romans 14:17 –

A familiar prayer in Scripture is "Thy kingdom come"
(Matt. 6:9-13). As we wait for His kingdom to be
established on the earth in the future, God is establishing
His kingdom within His people today.

Romans 14:17 tells us that the kingdom of God within us is being established through the person of the Holy
Spirit. Our problems come when we try to establish
God's kingdom in our lives through our own efforts
or systems. We cannot produce or establish anything
that is of God.

There are three things the Holy Spirit works within
us to establish God's kingdom: righteousness, peace,
and joy. It is the work of the Holy Spirit to produce all
three. God does not want one-third of His kingdom
established within us, or two-thirds, but the whole. The
Kingdom does not come within us in sections or on the
installment plan. God doesn't say, "Be good and I will
give you righteousness. Be very good for a long time
and I will give you peace. Be very, very good for a long,
long time and I will give you joy."

His Kingdom within You (II)

The Scribes and Pharisees who lived during the years of Jesus' ministry were a group of outwardly religious people who went about trying to establish their own righteousness through their works and by keeping their man-made rules and traditions. They worked hard at it, but it did not produce any joy or peace within them. Instead, they were without faith, hard, demanding, angry, critical, and judgmental. Their outward form of righteousness left them empty. And, when they were confronted with the reality of the kingdom of God through Jesus Christ, they became more miserable.

We cannot walk in daily peace and joy if we carry unrighteousness in our hearts. The unrighteousness of bitterness, resentment, and unforgiveness will rob us of our peace and joy; the unrighteousness of worry, fear, and anxiety will quench the flow of the Holy Spirit within us. Everything about righteousness is good, pure, clean, wholesome, and healthy to our inner-man. Attitudes of unrighteousness will quench the peace and joy of the Holy Spirit, but righteousness will release them. The fruit of righteousness is not sour grapes.

His Kingdom within You (III)

Inward righteousness comes from the Holy Spirit,
    not disciplines or rituals.
Inward peace comes from the Holy Spirit,
    not from ideal circumstances or times of silence.
Inward joy comes from the Holy Spirit,
    not from entertainment or good times.

As believers in Jesus Christ we need to yield to the Holy Spirit and allow Him to produce the life of the Kingdom within us. Let Him anoint you with the oil of joy and clothe you with the garment of praise; let His peace rule in your heart and guard your mind; let His righteousness bring health and wholeness to your spirit. Today, may your prayer be, "Lord, let Your kingdom come ... in me."

Divine Guidance

It's good to remember that our choices are not based upon what is the easiest thing for us to do, or what is the most comfortable thing for us to do. Our choices are based upon what God asks us to do, not about the outcome. Obedience is our choice to the revealed will of God, the results of our obedience are in God's hands. Jesus never said "follow success" and He never said "follow failure" He said "follow Me."

Whatsoever, whensoever wheresoever, Thou pleasest!

– R. M. M'CHEYNE

We say – God intends me to be here because I am so useful. Jesus never estimated His life along the line of the greatest use. God puts His saints where they will glorify Him, and we are no judges at all of where that is.

– OSWALD CHAMBERS

His Life, His Love

The trees of the LORD are full of sap.

– PSALM 104:16

Without sap the tree cannot flourish or even exist. Vitality is essential to a Christian. There must be life – a vital principle infused into us by God the Holy Spirit – or we cannot be trees of the Lord. What a secret thing the sap is! The roots go searching through the soil, but we cannot see them transform the mineral into the vegetable. This work is done down in the dark. Our root is Christ Jesus, and our life is hid in Him. This is the secret of the Lord. In the Christian, the divine life is always full of energy.

– CHARLES H. SPURGEON

I follow where Thou leadest, what are bruises?
There are cool leaves of healing on Thy tree;
Lead Thou me on. Thy heavenly wisdom chooses
In love for me.
Thy lover then, like happy homing swallow
That crosses hill and plain and lonely sea,
All unafraid, so I will fearless follow,
For love of Thee.

– AMY CARMICHAEL

Rescued (I)

It was dusk when I decided to hook up with one more wave before calling it a day. I was stretched out, face down on my surfboard, as I worked my way toward deeper water. As I lazily floated on the water I lifted my head and noticed that the beach seemed much further away then I remembered it being a few moments earlier. I started to paddle, hoping to move my surfboard closer to land; however, instead of moving forward, I continued to drift further out to sea.

I paddled harder, but the beach only grew more distant. At that moment, I realized I was caught in the pull of a riptide. With the sun setting I knew that it wouldn't be long before I would be heading out to sea in complete darkness. In desperation I cried out to God, "Help me!" In an instant, from out of nowhere, I saw a wave forming behind me. It caught my board with a mighty thrust and carried me all the way to the shore. I knew, beyond a doubt, it was the hand of God.

This is a true story. Sometimes, the best prayer you can pray is, "Lord, help me!"

Rescued (II)

A riptide is a strong surface flow of water returning seaward from near the shore. It can be extremely dangerous, dragging people away from the beach and leading to possible death as they attempt to fight the current and become exhausted. Hundreds of people are rescued from their clutches each year.

I believe there are spiritual riptides that can be a danger to our walk with Jesus Christ. Sometimes they can be subtle and go unseen, but once we are in their grip, they can pull us away from our peace, our joy, and our confident trust in the Lord.

Riptides are stronger when the surf is rough as the result of a storm. When we go through rough times and difficult circumstances, the pull of the enemy can be the strongest. He can attack our minds with thoughts of fear, anxiety, doubt and worry. These thoughts can work like riptides as they try to bring us into the deep waters of discouragement, depression, or despair.

Rescued (III)

Riptides are also stronger when the tide is low. We need to guard our hearts whenever we sense we are emotionally or physically down. If we are not careful, we can be swept into the enemy's riptide of lies when we are overworked, exhausted, physically weak, or going through great stress or disappointment.

If you sense you have been pulled into the enemy's riptide, do not panic; do not try and fight your way out in your own strength. Instead, cry out to the Lord and ask Him to deliver you.

In Psalm 34:6 we read, "This poor man cried, and the Lord heard him, and saved him out of all his troubles." The Lord is your deliverer, your redeemer, your rescuer, your lifeguard. He is mighty to save; He will rescue you and keep you from going under.

Casting Your Cares on Him

Casting all your care upon Him,
for He cares for you.
– 1 Peter 5:7 –

How do you cast your cares upon the Lord? Perhaps this fishing analogy will help you take the steps needed to release them all.

1. Get out your "fishing pole of faith".
2. Take all your cares and put the weight of them on a hook (the more the cares, the bigger the hook).
3. Tie the hook to the line on your fishing pole.
4. Cast the line as far as you can into the sea of God's faithfulness.
5. Cut the line to make sure you don't reel back any of your cares.

He Has Overcome the World

I have told you these things, so that in Me you may have [perfect] peace and confidence. In the world you have tribulation and trials and distress and frustration; but be of good cheer [take courage; be confident, certain, undaunted]! For I have overcome the world. [I have deprived it of power to harm you and have conquered it for you].
– John 16:33 AMP –

Your heart can be thankful today because:

- God is in control;
- He is on the throne;
- He is wise and good;
- He has made you complete in Him;
- He knows His own;
- He knows what He is doing;
- He has your life in His hands;
- He is working out His plan;
- He has overcome the world!

A Servant Leader

*"You know that the rulers in this world lord it
over their people, and officials flaunt their authority
over those under them. But among you it will be
different. Whoever wants to be a leader among you
must be your servant, and whoever wants to be first
among you must be the slave of everyone else. For
even the Son of Man came not to be served but to
serve others and to give His life as a ransom for many."*
– Mark 10:42-45 NLT –

A servant-leader is Someone who:

- can set direction and inspire, instead of being bossy;
- makes others successful, instead of using them for his advancement;
- is genuine, instead of a manipulator;
- motivates through encouragement, instead of through fear;
- takes time to listen, instead of being set in his ways;
- builds others up, instead of picking them apart;
- creates loyalty, instead of mistrust;
- imparts vision and unity, instead of confusion and dissension.

When the Answer is "No"

*Now this is the confidence that
we have in Him, that if we ask anything
according to His will, He hears us.*
– 1 John 5:14 –

It's good to have a smart car. A smart car won't let you lock the doors if you don't take the key out of the ignition. It's nice to have a car that's smart enough to keep you from doing something that dumb! In a way, a smart car refuses to answer your request because it knows that if it did, you would be in a much more difficult situation.

When we come to God with certain petitions, we can be eternally grateful that sometimes His answer is "no." It is important for us to understand that His "no" is not based upon our lack of sincerity, but upon the greatness of His wisdom. He is much too wise to say "yes" to any prayer that would bring us more harm than good if it were granted.

Characteristics of a Servant According to God's Heart (I)

1. The presence of the Lord rests upon his life.
2. He speaks with power and authority.
3. He loves what God loves.
4. He seeks God's purposes.
5. He's fearful of displeasing God.
6. He inspires trust.
7. His word is true.
8. He is deeply identified with God's feelings.
9. He is the same with everyone.
10. He does not minister legalism or licentiousness.
11. He is wise in his walk.
12. He takes people beyond themselves.
13. He despises anything that hurts others.
14. He proclaims his dependence on God.
15. He is well balanced.

Characteristics of a Servant According to God's Heart (II)

16. He is efficient, but not at the cost of others.
17. His life is in order.
18. Jesus is his audience.
19. He knows how to bear injustice.
20. He loves the truth.
21. His goal is to know God, and make Him known to others.
22. He is not satisfied if he doesn't give his best.
23. He is an optimist, not a pessimist.
24. His greatest passion is Jesus.
25. He delights in giving.
26. Others say of him "That is how my God is."
27. He doesn't exploit others.
28. He respects other servants.
29. He is always learning.
30. His convictions are firm, although he can be flexible.
31. He loves being nothing.

– DON LESSIN, AUTHOR OF *ABBA CRY*

One Way to Stop Worrying

There once was a man who worried all the time.

One day a friend noticed that he had stopped worrying.

"How did you do it?" the friend asked.

"It's simple; I hired a man to do all my worrying for me."

"How much did that cost you?"

"I agreed to pay him a thousand dollars a week."

"How can you pay him? You only make five hundred dollars a week."

"Well, I guess that's his worry!"

March

Receiving and Giving His Love

Let me tell you what real surrender is. It is simply resting in the love of God, as a little baby rests in its mother's arms.

– FRANÇOIS FENÉLON

We are not often called to great sacrifice, but daily we are presented with the chance to make small ones – a chance to make someone cheerful, a chance to do some small thing to make someone comfortable or contented, a chance to lay down our petty preferences or cherished plans. This requires us to relinquish something – our own convenience or comfort, our own free evening, our warm fireside, or even our habitual shyness, reserve or pride.

– ELISABETH ELLIOT

Faith

*Faith is the confidence that what we hope for
will actually happen; it gives us assurance about
things we cannot see. It is impossible to please
God without faith. Anyone who wants to come
to Him must believe that God exists and that
He rewards those who sincerely seek Him.*
– Hebrews 11:1, 6 NLT –

The eyes of Faith can see what your physical eyes can never see.

The knowing of Faith goes beyond what your natural mind can ever comprehend.

The possession of Faith receives what your physical arms can never embrace.

Your faith in God is your lifeline to His heartbeat; it is the hand that reaches up and takes hold of God's promises. It gathers in the spiritual treasures that are found in Christ. It stands upon what is sure and certain. It rests in what is unfailing. It says "yes" to every promise that has been written. It moves forward with all confidence in a God who cannot fail.

"Setting the Table"

As I prepared to speak on the Feast of Tabernacles there were three things I wanted to focus upon:

1. The feast was a time of joyful celebration.
2. The feast had a strong emphasis upon water and the blessings of rain.
3. The feast was a time of thanksgiving for God's abundant provisions.

Before I spoke, three people had a Scripture they wanted to share with the congregation. The first Scripture focused on "joy". The second Scripture focused on "water". The third Scripture focused on "God's bounty". I was totally amazed to think that each one was led to read a Scripture that covered one of the things I wanted to share about the feast.

I could only smile as I thought about what God had done to prepare the hearts of His people. It was His way of "setting the table" for what He had for them that evening.

I wonder how God will be "setting the table" for you to receive what He has for you to feast upon today?

Our Response to God (I)

I don't understand the thinking that says it's okay to be angry at God. It makes me wonder what people are angry about. God has never made a blunder, never made a mistake, and has never done anything wrong. There are no flaws in God's character.

Job was a man who went through great trials, hardship, and suffering. When his wife told him to curse God and die, Job refused. What Job did say was, "You speak as a foolish woman. Shall we indeed accept good from God, and shall we not accept adversity?" (Job. 2:8-10) The Bible goes on to tell us, "In all this Job did not sin with his lips."

How could anyone be angry at Someone who is perfect, who is all wise, who is love, who is altogether good, who is holy, who never sins, who never does evil, who never lies, and who has promised never to leave us or forsake us.

Our Response to God (II)

Is anger ever appropriate? Of course! We should be angry at sin, at the works of darkness, at the powers of hell, at evil, at unrighteousness, and at our own selfishness and rebellion.

To be angry at anything but what displeases God is to displease God in being angry.

— WILLIAM BEVERIDGE

We know that we shall at once lose the light of discernment, and the security of good counsel, and our very uprightness, and the temperate character of righteousness, if the main light of our heart has been darkened (by the shadow of anger): next, that the purity of our soul will presently be clouded, and that it cannot possibly be made a temple for the Holy Ghost while the spirit of anger resides in us; lastly, that we should consider that we ought never to pray, nor pour out our prayer to God, while we are angry.

— SAINT JOHN CASSIAN

Our Response to God (III)

Instead of anger, the Bible reveals several important ways we can come into God's presence.

Awe
When Joshua met the Captain of the host of the Lord (Josh. 5:13-15) he was told, "Remove your sandals from your feet, for the place where you are standing is holy."

When Moses approached the burning bush (Exod. 3:5) he was told, "Remove your sandals from your feet, for the place on which you are standing is holy ground."

When Isaiah saw the Lord sitting on His throne (Isa. 6:1-5) he saw His holiness and cried, "Woe is me."

When John saw the glory of the Lord (Rev. 1:17) he fell at His feet like one who was dead.

We must never lose the awe of God. To see Him is to carry a sense of wonder and dread, amazement and respect, worship and fear. The thought of coming into the presence of God should leave us speechless.

Our Response to God (IV)

Thankfulness
In Colossians 3, Paul reminds the believers to, "Be thankful. Giving thanks to God the Father through Him."

In 1 Thessalonians 5:18 (AMP) Paul says, "Thank [God] in everything [no matter what the circumstances may be, be thankful and give thanks], for this is the will of God for you [who are] in Christ Jesus [the Revealer and Mediator of that will].

In Psalm 100:4 we are told, "Enter into His gates with thanksgiving and a thank offering and into His courts with praise! Be thankful and say so to Him."

In Timothy we read, "In the last days ... people will be ... ungrateful." We live in an ungrateful world. To listen to most, you would think that either God didn't exist, or if He did, that He was indifferent, unkind, and uncaring.

God's generosity to us in Jesus Christ is overwhelming – God gives us a clean heart, a joyful heart, a loving heart, a peaceful heart – yet, there is one thing God cannot give us, and that is a thankful heart. Thankfulness is our gift to Him.

Our Response to God (V)

Praise
In the midst of difficulty, Peter told believers, "In this you greatly rejoice, though now for a little while, if need be, you have been grieved by various trials." (1 Peter 1:6.)

The psalmist tells us to, "Serve the Lord with gladness" (Ps. 100:2). "His praise shall continually be in our mouth" (Ps. 34:1).

There is never a time when God is not worthy of praise. Nothing about Him ever changes, even in the midst of our most difficult days He is still faithful, still true, still on the throne, and still working out His plan.

God never promised us an easy life or one that would be free of trials, hardships and suffering. These things should not surprise us if we are following His ways. We know Jesus learned obedience by the things He suffered, and for the joy that was set before Him, He endured the cross. The apostle Paul went through great difficulties, yet he said he would gladly suffer the loss of all things to gain Christ.

Our Response to God (VI)

A heart that gives thanks in everything, that rejoices evermore, and that is broken and humble before Him is a heart that gladdens the heart of God.

Here are some keys to walking before God with a thankful, rejoicing, worshipful heart.

- If you have been hurt, walk in forgiveness.
- If you have enemies, bless them and pray for them.
- If you have been disappointed, give all your expectations to God.
- If you are being disciplined, do not despise the correction of the Lord.
- If your pride has been wounded, humble yourself before the mighty hand of God.
- If you are struggling with your own way, take up your cross and follow Jesus.
- If you are burdened, worried or fearful, cast all your cares upon Him.

Skilled

Do you see a man diligent and skillful in
his business? He will stand before kings,
– Proverbs 22:29 AMP –

The word *diligent* can mean skilled or ready. Diligent is another way of saying that it is important to be prepared. Abraham Lincoln said, "I will prepare myself and then my opportunity will come." Leonard Ravenhill said, "The opportunity of a lifetime must be seized within the lifetime of the opportunity."

It is important that you do your work well, but it is also important to be growing in your work and in your skills. Don't settle for "just getting by." Continue to find ways to grow, to expand your learning, and to improve your skills.

Lord, thank You for the gifts and abilities You have given me. Thank You that I can serve You with my heart and my skills in the workplace. Show me new ways to learn and to grow. Keep me fresh and ever growing. I want to always be in a place of readiness and willingness to serve and honor You.

Amen.

God Has Plans

Corrie ten Boom once said, "God has no problems, only plans."

God doesn't make bad days for you and good days for you. God makes each day fit perfectly into His plans for you. Here are some promises for you to trust in:

"For I know the thoughts and plans
that I have for you, says the Lord, thoughts
and plans for welfare and peace and not for evil,
to give you hope in your final outcome."
– Jeremiah 29:11 AMP –

[As for me] I am poor and needy, yet the Lord
takes thought and plans for me. You are my Help
and my Deliverer. O my God, do not tarry!
– Psalm 40:17 AMP –

A man's heart plans his way,
but the LORD directs his steps.
– Proverbs 16:9 –

Peace Is Not Based on Reason

Anxiety in the heart of man causes depression.
– Proverbs 12:25 AMP –

Anxiety cannot abide in your heart when God's peace comes. It is a peace your reason cannot explain. You cannot 'reason' peace into your heart. Peace comes because God gives it to you. Your circumstances may be anything but peaceful, yet His peace can abide within you.

Is there something you are anxious about? If you are depressed, ask God to reveal the cause. It is possible that the root cause is anxiety.

The Financial World (I)

Receive my instruction in preference to
[striving for] silver, and knowledge rather
than choice gold, for skillful and godly Wisdom
is better than rubies or pearls, and all the things
that may be desired are not to be compared to it.
– Proverbs 8:10-11 AMP –

As we experience the ups and downs of the financial world, many wonder what it all means and where we are going. The financial world, when the signs are bad, can bring confusion, bewilderment, fear, and panic to the hearts of people.

As the financial world goes through constant change, it is important for us to remember that the quiet place God has for us has not gone away.

God's peace is not tumbling with the stock market;
God's rest is not vanishing before our eyes;
God's hope is not being devalued;
God's grace has not been depleted;
God's riches in Christ have not gone bankrupt.

The love, goodness, and mercies of God are never inflated or overvalued.

The Financial World (II)

C. S. Lewis writes,

> If the first and lowest operation of pain shatters the illusion that all is well, the second shatters the illusion that what we have is our own and enough for us. We 'have all we want' is a terrible saying when 'all' does not include God. Now God, who has made us, knows what we are and that our happiness is in Him. Yet we will not seek it in Him as long as He leaves us any other resort where it can even plausibly be looked for. While what we call 'our own life' remains agreeable we will not surrender it to Him. What then can God do in our interests but make 'our own life' less agreeable to us, and take away the plausible source of false happiness.

The 'pain' that comes from the financial world is a powerful reminder that if we place our trust and our security in anything or anyone but God alone, we can see it crumble before our eyes. If we can quiet our hearts we will hear the sound of God's still small voice drawing us to Himself, assuring us of His presence, and saying, "Peace be still."

Teach Us to Pray

Matthew 6:9-13

Our Father	HIS PERSON
Which art in heaven	HIS POSITION
Hallowed be Thy Name	HIS PRE-EMINENCE
Thy Kingdom come	HIS POWER
Thy will be done	HIS PURPOSE
On earth as it is in heaven	HIS PATTERN
Give us this day our daily bread	HIS PROVISION
Forgive us our debts	HIS PARDON
Lead us not into temptation	HIS PROTECTION
but deliver us from evil	
For Thine is the Kingdom,	HIS PRAISE
and the power,	
and glory, forever.	
Amen	

– DAVID RAVENHILL

"I Am" (I)

God replied to Moses, "I AM WHO I AM. Say this
to the people of Israel: I AM has sent me to you."
– Exodus 3:14 NLT –

Jesus answered, "I tell you the truth, before Abraham was even born, I AM!" (John 8:58 NLT).

God used the burning bush to draw Moses aside, to hear God's voice and to discover how God wanted to use him. What Moses heard was God's plan, not Moses' plan. God does not come to us and ask, "What is it you would like to do with your life? Just let me know and I will back you all the way." It is God's plan that we must follow.

When Moses heard what God was calling him to do he immediately began to look at his resources instead of God's. Moses' focus was on what he couldn't do instead of on what God could do. God did not say to him, "Come on Moses, you can do it. You can do anything if you just put your mind to it." What God wanted Moses to understand was that God was the one who would fulfill Moses' calling. It was okay for Moses to say, "I can't", but he also needed to say, "You can!"

"I Am" (II)

Let the burning bush be a reminder to you of God's call and plan. He is the one who has called you and will equip you. He is the one who sends you and goes before you. He is the one who is your wisdom, your authority, and your confidence. He is your great "I Am."

As the "I Am" He is the God of the past, the God of the future, and the God of today. He never says, "What I once have been I can no longer be." He never says, "What I will be in the future I cannot be today." God is always in the "eternal now." All that He was He always will be.

When God says "I Am" He is saying that He is all-in-all. He is your provider and He is your provision, whatever your need may be.

In trouble, He is your peace;
    In lack, He is your sufficiency;
In changing circumstances, He is your contentment;
    In difficulty, He is your joy;
In weakness, He is your strength;
    In battle, He is your victory;
In impossibilities, He is your miracle worker.

Diligence

He becomes poor who works with a slack and
idle hand, but the hand of the diligent makes rich.
– Proverbs 10:4 AMP –

One of the flaws in education is placing a strong emphasis on grades and not on character. A person can graduate college with academic honors and be morally bankrupt. Poor character impacts every area of our lives, especially the workplace. Many times employers say, "It's so hard to find good help who know how to work."

In the apprenticeship system, young people grew up learning a trade and learning how to work with their hands. Children who grew up on farms often learned that playtime was a privilege, not a right. Everyone who has a job has a choice to make. He can either be slack in his work or diligent. Employers notice the difference and reward those whose work is honest and noble.

Jesus, teach me to work as You worked. Show me what it means to be persistent and hard-working. I want to have the consistent joy of going home each day knowing I have put in a good day's work and have done my best.

Amen.

What's It All About?

It's about the painting, not the frame;
  It's about the treasure, not the vessel;
It's about His truth, not our opinions;
  It's about His glory, not our looks;
It's about His love, not our niceness;
  It's about His purpose, not our plans;
It's about His kingdom, not our agenda;
  It's about His reign, not our rights;
It's about His life, not our efforts.
  It's about Jesus!

*But we all, with unveiled face, beholding
as in a mirror the glory of the Lord, are being
transformed into the same image from glory to
glory, just as by the Spirit of the Lord.*
– 2 Corinthians 3:18 –

*For it is the God who commanded light to
shine out of darkness, who has shone in our
hearts to give the light of the knowledge of the
glory of God in the face of Jesus Christ. But we
have this treasure in earthen vessels.*
– 2 Corinthians 4:6-7 –

It's Good to Wait upon His Promises

Wait for the promise of the Father.
– Acts 1:4 –

And the peace of God, which surpasses
all understanding, will guard your hearts
and minds through Christ Jesus.
– Philippians 4:7 –

Tarry at a promise till God meets you there. He always returns by way of His promise.

– DWIGHT L. MOODY

If you find that you are anxious about something ask yourself if you have prayed about it, and fully committed it to the Lord.

If you have prayed about it, committed it to the Lord, and are still anxious, begin to thank God in your heart and in your prayers for being in control of the situation. Prayer, commitment, and thanksgiving open the door to peace as you wait for His answer.

The World and the Kingdom (I)

*Your kingdom come, Your will be
done on earth as it is in heaven.*
– Matthew 6:10 AMP –

The world pursues mammon; the Kingdom pursues God.

The world uses people; the Kingdom serves people.

The world seeks to please man; the Kingdom seeks to please God.

The world uses God to advance personal interests; the Kingdom obeys God to advance His interests.

The world looks for significance in titles, recognition and advancement; the Kingdom brings significance because of the value God places upon each individual, regardless of personal status.

The world operates with fear and manipulation to get people to perform; the Kingdom operates with love that motivates people to please.

The world brings bondage; the Kingdom brings freedom.

The World and the Kingdom (II)

The world creates a parting spirit that puts down others; the Kingdom creates a gracious spirit that builds others up.

The world is about gaining personal success; the Kingdom is about making others successful.

The world seeks after power and control; the Kingdom seeks after meekness and yielding to God's control.

The world steals from others and takes credit for someone else's work; the Kingdom honors others and seeks their highest good.

The world wears a mask and walks in dishonesty; the Kingdom is real and walks in truth.

The world criticizes the competition and actively tries to hurt them; the Kingdom gives honor where honor is due and seeks to bless.

The world is interested in the dollar that is in the consumer's wallet; the Kingdom is interested in the need that is in the consumer's heart.

Wholeness

God wants you to be whole, in body, in soul, and in spirit. He wants you to be fully complete in Him, without any gaps, holes, or empty places in your heart. He that fills all in all wants to fill all of you with all He has to give.

For she said within herself, If I may but
touch His garment, I shall be whole.
– Matthew 9:21 KJV –

But Jesus turned Him about, and when
He saw her, he said, Daughter, be of good comfort;
thy faith hath made thee whole. And the
woman was made whole from that hour.
– Matthew 9:22 KJV –

"They that are whole have no need of the
physician, but they that are sick."
– Mark 2:16-17 KJV –

"The Spirit of the Lord is upon me ... He hath
sent me to heal the brokenhearted, to preach
deliverance to the captives, and recovering of sight
to the blind, to set at liberty them that are bruised.
–Luke 4:18 KJV –

Health

Healing is a blessing from God and so is good health. In so many ways, God expresses His grace and mercies to you, touching you in your need, time and time again. He renews your strength, restores your well-being, revives your heart, refreshes your spirit, and relaxes your nerves.

Bless the LORD, O my soul: and all that is within me, bless His holy name. Bless the LORD, O my soul, and forget not all His benefits: Who forgiveth all thine iniquities; who healeth all thy diseases.
– Psalm 103:1-3 KJV –

Why art thou cast down, O my soul? And why art thou disquieted within me? Hope thou in God: for I shall yet praise Him, who is the health of my countenance, and my God.
– Psalm 42:11 KJV –

Be not wise in thine own eyes: fear the LORD, and depart from evil. It shall be health to thy navel, and marrow to thy bones.
– Proverbs 3:7-8 KJV –

More Than Enough

The chariots of God are twenty thousand,
even thousands of angels: the Lord is
among them, as in Sinai, in the holy place.
– Psalm 68:17 KJV –

The resources of God that He sends on your behalf are more than enough to bring you through each day triumphantly. If one angel is not enough, God will send two. If two are not enough, God will send ten thousand.

God Watches Over You

Under His wings shalt thou trust: His truth
shall be thy shield and buckler.
– Psalm 91:4 KJV –

Have no fears or worries,
Simply be at rest –
Trusting in your Father,
He knows what is best.

His love rests upon you,
Angels are everywhere –
Your heart can be certain
You are in His care.

Clothing, food, and shelter
His love freely brings –
Faithfully He'll keep you
Covered by His wings.

Everything He's promised
He will surely do –
God, Who sees the sparrow
Watches over you.

You Are Not ...

Thou, even Thou, art LORD alone;
Thou hast made heaven, the heaven of heavens,
with all their host, the earth, and all things
that are therein, the seas, and all that is therein,
and Thou preservest them all; and the
host of heaven worshippeth Thee.
– Nehemiah 9:6 KJV –

You are not alone –
 For God is with you.
You are not defenseless –
 For God is your protector.
 You are not inadequate –
For God is your sufficiency.
 You are not useless –
For God has a purpose for you.
 You are not hopeless –
For God is your future.
 You are not unaccepted, rejected, or abandoned –
For God loves you with an everlasting love.

Grace

God is full of grace. What a wonderful word grace is to us, what a wonderful gift it is in us, what a glorious provision it is for us. Today, take a few moments and soak in the truth of His grace ...

For the Lord God is a sun and shield: the Lord will give grace and glory: no good thing will He withhold from them that walk uprightly.
– Psalm 84:11 KJV –

And the Word was made flesh, and dwelt among us, (and we beheld His glory, the glory as of the only begotten of the Father,) full of grace and truth.
– John 1:14 KJV –

From the fullness of His grace we have all received one blessing after another.
– John 1:16 NIV –

And now, brethren, I commend you to God, and to the word of His grace, which is able to build you up, and to give you an inheritance among all them which are sanctified.
– Acts 20:32 KJV –

Grace Upon Grace

Gods' grace is poured upon you – the grace of His acceptance, the grace of His favor, the grace of His pleasure, the grace of His liberty. Soak again today in more of God's amazing grace.

My grace is sufficient for thee: for My strength is made perfect in weakness. Most gladly therefore will I rather glory in my infirmities, that the power of Christ may rest upon me.
– 2 Corinthians 12:9 KJV –

Now our Lord Jesus Christ Himself, and God, even our Father, which hath loved us, and hath given us everlasting consolation and good hope through grace.
– 2 Thessalonians 2:16 KJV –

Thou therefore, my son, be strong in the grace that is in Christ Jesus.
– 2 Timothy 2:1 KJV –

Let us therefore come boldly unto the throne of grace, that we may obtain mercy, and find grace to help in time of need.
– Hebrews 4:16 KJV –

You Can, Because He Can

*I know that You can do everything, and that
no purpose of Yours can be withheld from You.*
– Job 42:2 –

You can ask of the Lord
    because He will not give you a wrong answer.
You can wait upon the Lord
    because His timing is always perfect.
You can trust in the Lord
    because He makes no mistakes.
You can hope in the Lord
    because He holds your future.
You can rest in the Lord
    because He is in control of your life.
You can lean upon the Lord
    because He is completely faithful.

What to Do and Not to Do

Here are five things to be doing as you await Jesus' return:

- Be watchful.
- Be peaceful.
- Be prayerful.
- Be sober.
- Be ready.

Here are five things not to be doing as you await Jesus' return:

- Do not be fearful.
- Do not be deceived.
- Do not be troubled.
- Do not be spiritually asleep.
- Do not be weighed down with cares.

April

Why Jesus Died

When Jesus died upon the cross He didn't die as a martyr, He died as a sacrifice for sin. He didn't die for His sins, for He was without sin. He died to make atonement for us. He died so that each person who turns from his or her sin, and believes in Him, could be forgiven. He gave His life freely, and lovingly. God sent His Son because He loves you. Jesus shed His blood because He loves you. Jesus didn't die just for the world – He died for you. Do you know how much you are loved? You are loved with all the love that God could give.

Jesus took the judgment for our sin upon Himself so that we wouldn't have to be judged. He tasted death so that we wouldn't know the sting of death. He descended into hell so that we would never need to know its awful grip upon our lives. And after three days He rose from the grave so that we could know resurrection life.

There Was and There Will Be (I)

There was a time when Jesus entered the city of Jerusalem in a most unusual way (John 12).

There will be a time when Jesus returns to this earth in a most unusual way (1 Thess. 4:16).

There was a time when He rode upon a young donkey (John 12:14).

There will be a time when He rides upon a white horse (Rev. 19:11).

There was a time when He came as the Sacrificial Lamb (John 1:36).

There will be a time when He comes as the Righteous Judge (Rev. 19:11).

There was a time when He came humbly and lowly (Zech. 9:9).

There will be a time when He comes to conquer and make war (Rev. 19:11).

There Was and There Will Be (II)

There was a time when palm branches were cast before Him (John 12:13).

There will be a time when crowns will be cast before His throne (Rev. 4:10).

There was a time when people proclaimed, "Hosanna" (John 12:13).

There will be a time when people proclaim, "Blessing, and honor, and glory, and power, be unto Him" (Rev. 5:13).

There was a time when the local crowds cried out His praises (John 12:13).

There will be a time when people from every kindred, tongue, people, and nation will worship at His feet (Rev. 5:9).

There was a time when a multitude saw His triumphal entry (John 12:12).

There will be a time when everyone on earth will see His triumphal return (Rev. 1:7).

Jesus Died and Rose for You!

Jesus died and rose for you. Does this not say it all? The death and resurrection of Jesus Christ was in the Father's heart before the world was formed, before a flower bloomed, before a creature moved, before man walked in God's garden!

For all the sins you've committed, God says, "All is forgiven. By faith alone you are righteous in My sight because My Son died and rose for you." For all the things you've done to try and earn God's favor, He says, "Your righteousness will never be enough to save you or keep you. That is why My Son died and rose for you. By faith alone His righteousness can now be yours."

Does God Love You?

*God demonstrates His own love towards us
in that while we were still sinners, Christ died
for us. Much more then, having now been justified by
His blood, we shall be saved from wrath through Him.
For if when we were enemies we were reconciled to
God through the death of His Son, much more,
having been reconciled, we shall be saved by His life.*
– Romans 5:9-10 –

Does God love you?
    Yes, Jesus died and rose for you.
Does God care about you?
    Yes, Jesus died and rose for you.
Will God save you and restore you?
    Yes, Jesus died and rose for you.
Will God provide for you?
    Yes, Jesus died and rose for you.

All Is Yours

For all things are yours: whether ... the world or life or death, or things present or things to come – all are yours. And you are Christ's, and Christ is God's.
– 1 Corinthians 3:21-23 –

Jesus died and rose for you. If you only knew this one truth, it would be enough. If you only had this spiritual bread to eat it would sustain you.

If you only had this living water to drink it would quench your thirst. Yet, by His grace there is even more.

Jesus died and rose for you. Is this not the tap root from which the tree of life grows? Is this not the headwater from which the healing river flows? Is this not the pen from which all doctrine is written?

Does not justification, sanctification, redemption, and all the other truths of Scripture become yours because Jesus died and rose for you?

The answer is *yes*. Yes, a million times over! Your life in Him is now an all-encompassing "Yes" because Jesus died and rose for you. Today hope is yours, life is yours, heaven is yours, blessings upon blessings are yours, because Jesus died and rose for you.

Jesus' Cross and Empty Tomb

The cross means that we can look back and be thankful;
　　the empty tomb means that we can look ahead and be hopeful.

The cross fills us with gratitude;
　　the empty tomb fills us with expectation.

The cross means that He died for us;
　　the empty tomb means that He lives for us.

The cross means that the old has passed away;
　　the empty tomb means that all things have become new.

The cross is the triumph of mercy;
　　the empty tomb is the triumph of righteousness.

The message of the cross is, "It is finished";
　　the message of the empty tomb is, "I am alive forever more."

New Life

*Therefore, if anyone is in Christ, he is
a new creation; old things have passed away;
behold, all things have become new.*
– 2 Corinthians 5:17 –

When Jesus comes to live within us He brings brand-new life, like springtime to our hearts – the dark places in us are replaced with His glorious light, the cold places with His warmth, the barren places with His fruitfulness.

New things come alive in us. The warming wind of His Spirit makes us feel fresh and clean. Seeds of faith are planted in the rich soil of His promises. Blossoms of hope begin to shoot forth. Young fruit trees, with the sap of His character and ministry, begin to flow.

Springtime in our hearts beckons us on to growth – the seeds of faith need to be established, the blossoms of hope need to flower, and the fruit trees of His grace need to come to fruition. This new life leads us on – from faith to faith, from grace to grace, from glory to glory.

Jesus' Resurrection (I)

The resurrection allows us to look up, to look forward, and to look ahead.

When we look up we see Jesus seated at the right hand of God, when we look forward we see Him daily guiding our steps, when we look ahead we see Him coming again for His bride.

The resurrection of Jesus Christ brings the assurance that the enemy of death has been defeated, our home in heaven is secure, and our inheritance will never fade away. How good He is, and how blessed we are to serve a Lord who is alive, who is above all, and who loves us with an everlasting love!

Jesus' Resurrection (II)

His resurrection is our victory song, our shout of joy, our daily praise, and our eternal hope. Because He lives we shall live also. He has promised it. He has guaranteed it. He has secured it. Jesus is our life and heaven is our home. He is the perfect gift that we can know and enjoy forever.

The Resurrection of Jesus Christ (Matt. 28:5-7):

- **Calms Our Fears**
  The angel said to the women, "Do not be afraid, for I know that you are looking for Jesus, who was crucified. He is not here."
- **Confirms His Word**
  "He has risen, just as He said."
- **Comforts Our Hearts**
  "Come and see the place where He lay."
- **Commissions Our Lives**
  "Then go quickly and tell His disciples: 'He has risen from the dead and is going ahead of you into Galilee."
- **Clarifies Our Vision**
  "'There you will see Him.' Now I have told you."

His Life is Your Life

If there was no resurrection there wouldn't be:

- A Savior who could save,
- A King who could rule,
- A Shepherd who could lead,
- A Physician who could heal,
- A Provider who could supply,
- A Bridegroom who could love.

But because He lives there is:

- A Redeemer who forgives,
- A Lord who reigns,
- A Warrior who conquers,
- A High Priest who intercedes,
- A Counselor who guides,
- A Bridegroom who is coming for His bride.

When You Need Him Most

Can anything ever separate us from Christ's love?
Does it mean He no longer loves us if we have trouble
or calamity, or are persecuted, or hungry, or destitute,
or in danger, or threatened with death? ... No power in
the sky above or in the earth below – indeed, nothing in
all creation will ever be able to separate us from the
love of God that is revealed in Christ Jesus our Lord.
– Romans 8:35-39 NLT –

His strongest grace
    is for your weakest moment;
His sweetest fellowship
    is for your loneliest journey;
His richest supply
    is for your neediest hour;
His closest embrace
    is for your deepest sorrow;
His brightest light
    is for your darkest day.

The Assurance of His Presence

And the Word (Christ) became flesh (human,
incarnate) and tabernacled (fixed His tent
of flesh, lived awhile) among us; and we [actually]
saw His glory (His honor, His majesty), such glory
as an only begotten son receives from His father,
full of grace (favor, loving-kindness) and truth.
– John 1:14 AMP –

The meaning of "Tabernacle" reaches into the deepest places of our hearts. Its impact was first known to the people of Israel in the book of Exodus (28:43), was revealed to the early church through the Gospels (John 1:14), and is spoken of in the book of Revelation as an extension of God's loving care to His people in the final days (Rev. 7:15 AMP).

The word "Tabernacle" brings to us one of the clearest revelations of the love and care of God for His people. It says to us that God has chosen to come to us in our need, to draw close in intimacy and compassion, and to cover us with His presence.

The Comfort of His Presence

And I heard a loud voice from heaven saying,
"Behold, the tabernacle of God is with men, and He
will dwell with them, and they shall be His people.
God Himself will be with them and be their God."
– Revelation 21:3 –

When God's people go through great hardships and heartaches we often wonder what can be said that will bring true comfort and hope? One of things I believe we can say with strong affirmation is that God is there, in the midst of it all, drawing closer than any friend or family member ever could. This is at the heart of Jesus, our Tabernacle. Jesus didn't stay away from us, hiding from our sorrows in heaven; He came to us and tabernacled with us.

In the book of Revelation, God reaches out to those who have come through great tribulation and spreads His tabernacle over them – the tabernacle of His presence to protect and shelter them. In the midst of our deepest sorrows, tears, and struggles God spreads the tent of His presence over us!

God Is Close to You

And God will wipe away every tear from
their eyes; there shall be no more death, nor
sorrow, nor crying. There shall be no more pain,
for the former things have passed away.
– Revelation 21:4 –

How close is God to you when you face your greatest trials and difficulties? He is closer to you than anyone could ever be, and He does more for you than anyone could ever do.

The Bible tells us that God collects our tears in His bottle (Ps. 56:8), and that one day He will wipe away all tears from our eyes.

How close is God to you when your heart aches? He cannot collect your tears in His bottle and be standing at a distance. To be a collector of your tears, it means that God is not even an eyelash away.

There's No Place Like Home! (I)

"If anyone loves Me, he will keep My word;
and My Father will love him, and We will come
to him and make Our home with him."
– John 14:23 –

The Man Without a Country is a sad story that tells the plight of Philip Nolan, who renounced the United States of America and was sentenced to spend the rest of his life on warships of the United States Navy, without the right to ever again set foot on U.S. soil or hear its name mentioned.

One of the saddest stories in real life is the plight of the homeless who live on city streets and parks throughout the country. These are people with a thousand different stories to tell, but who all have one thing in common, the absence of a place they can call "home."

The saddest story of all is to learn of someone who is spiritually homeless. There is no greater emptiness, loneliness, or isolation than this. Jesus Christ came to make His home within our hearts. His presence makes it possible for every person to find their true home and their eternal home with Him.

There's No Place Like Home! (II)

Here are six characteristics of the home that Jesus wants to establish within us.

1. *A home of love* ... where His arms are extended to help, to support, to encourage, and to embrace.
2. *A home of acceptance* ... where you are valued, celebrated, enjoyed, and appreciated.
3. *A home of protection* ... where you can be sheltered from the coming storm and find safety from the heat of day, the cold of night, and the battering winds that beat against your life.
4. *A home of fellowship* ... where your heart can open up to Him, where feelings can be expressed, where thoughts can be exchanged; where deep touches deep, and soul touches soul in harmony, in unity, and in sweet communion.
5. *A home of light* ... where a glow fills the hallways and floods the rooms with welcomed illumination; where it is possible to clearly find your way and fully discover the treasures within.
6. *A home of warmth* ... where the fire of His presence burns brightly; its beauty drawing you close – bringing laughter, shared joys, while the golden flames of mercy and grace warm the deepest chills within.

Work and Rest (I)

*"Six days you shall work, but on the
seventh day you shall rest; in plowing
time and in harvest you shall rest."*
– Exodus 34:21 –

Work is a good thing. Work is in the will of God. It is a way we honor and obey God. Work is a blessing.

Work makes us active, productive, and useful instead of passive, idle, and dependent upon others. It provides a way of expressing our gifts and talents, it inspires creativity, it helps to develop character, it brings new relationships into our lives, and it gives us the satisfaction of doing a job to the very best of our ability.

When we receive and recognize that our work is a gift from God we have no reason to grumble and complain about our work.

Work and Rest (II)

It is also good to remember that the God who wants us to work also wants us to rest. Even though His will is for us to work, He does not want us to be consumed with our work or to have our work consume us. Rest is another way of reminding us that God is reasonable and considerate. He does not treat us like machines, but like people who have physical, mental, and emotional limitations. In God's plan, one day of rest will refresh our spirits, renew our minds, and restore to us the strength we will need for the week ahead.

Lord, thank You for the wisdom of Your ways. Thank You that You know what is best for me. Thank You for giving me the strength to work and the opportunity to do it. Help me to work when I work, and to rest when I rest. Bring my life into a proper balance and help me to keep a quiet heart in all I do.

Amen.

Prepared by Omnipotent Love

Our Christian life today is a foretaste of the heavenly banquet still to come; for God has "made us to sit down with Him" who first was seated by mighty power in the heavenly places far above all (Eph. 1:20; 2:6). This means that the work of salvation is not ours but His. It is not that we work for God but that He has worked for us. God gives us our position of rest. He brings His Son's finished work and presents it to us, and then He says to us, "Please sit."

His offer of salvation cannot, I think, be better expressed than in the words of invitation to the great feast in the parable: "Come; for all things are now ready."

– WATCHMAN NEE

You are His ... by conquest. What a battle He had in us before we were won! How long He laid siege to our walls against Him. But we have become the conquered captives of His omnipotent love. Thus chosen, purchased, and subdued, the rights of our divine Possessor are inalienable.

– CHARLES H. SPURGEON

Will the "Real You" Please Stand Up! (I)

Do you know who you really are in Jesus Christ? Have you discovered your true identity and are you living in the reality of it today? Years ago there was a TV game show called *To Tell the Truth*. During the show three contestants, each claiming the same identity, stood before a panel of judges. The object of the show was to see if the panel, by asking a series of questions to the contestants, could identify who was telling the truth. After the panel members made their guess, the host of the show would say, "Will the real .... please stand up."

If you do not know who you are Christ, you will not be able to "stand up" to your true identity. Because you are in Christ, you cannot let the devil try to tag you with a false identity.

You are the Lord's person and possession. He made you and He owns you. He has ownership of you through creation and redemption. Isn't it good to know that you are doubly His! You are no small thing to Him and your life is no small matter in His loving hands.

Will the "Real You" Please Stand Up! (II)

*"Fear not, for I have redeemed you; I have
called you by your name; you are Mine."*
– Isaiah 43:1 –

You are the Lord's, wholly and completely. There are no doubts in His mind or in heaven's records. The devil has no lien against your life. Because of the purchase price that Jesus paid upon the cross, Satan has no rightful claim upon you. He cannot approach the courts of heaven and say, "The shed blood of Jesus Christ was not payment enough to claim this life. I still am owed back payment and I refuse to release my legal rights."

Satan also has no parental right over you. The devil is not your father and he cannot say, "This is my child and I have every right to my authority over him." You are now God's child. You have been adopted into God's family. He is your Father and you are a joint-heir with Jesus Christ.

In Jesus Christ, there are no ties to your past to pull you back; no fears to hold you back; no chains to keep you back.

Will the "Real You" Please Stand Up! (III)

*"Therefore if the Son makes you free,
you shall be free indeed."*
– John 8:36 –

The Son has set you free, you are a new creation, the old has passed away and the new has come. Refuse every lie that places you outside of Christ. Forget the former things, for God has done a new thing in your life. You are not a victim who is held captive by the past, your circumstances, or your upbringing. Don't live in the past, for you have died to it all and your life is now hid with Christ in God.

Don't every say, "Poor me." Instead, say, "Rich me!" Jesus became poor so you could become rich. You have been lavished with riches – riches of grace, riches of mercy, riches of kindness, riches of love, riches of salvation, riches of glory for now and forevermore.

There is no reason to live a defeated life because Jesus is your life, and He is the victorious warrior. Be free, for Jesus has freed you; live free, for Jesus is your freedom. He is your life, and as He is so are you in this present world.

Ministry

Paul, a bondservant of Jesus Christ, called to be
an apostle, separated to the gospel of God.
– Romans 1:1 –

We don't have a ministry because we decide to have one; we have a ministry because God gives us one. Our calling, our work, and the fruit that comes from it is God's doing, not ours.

Our privilege is to obey what God tells us to do; our responsibility is to serve Him faithfully in the place of obedience, whether it is a hidden place or a public place. His blessing and His anointing comes to us when we are living in agreement with His will. We cannot manufacture God's blessing and anointing simply by being ambitious, highly motivated, or hard working.

The anointing and blessing of God comes through the work of the Holy Spirit, not through our own efforts. An ounce of obedience is worth more than a pound of strife and a ton of self-effort.

The Palms of His Hands

"See, I have inscribed you on
the palms of My hands."
– Isaiah 49:16 –

When God looks at the palms of His hands what does He see? He sees you!

Let the following words from Charles H. Spurgeon encourage you today:

God keeps His promise a thousand times, but the trial makes us doubt Him. He never fails. He is never a dry well. Yet, we are as continually vexed with anxieties, molested with suspicions, and disturbed with fears as if our God were the mirage of the desert … you are written on the palms of His hands. It does not say, "your name." The name is there, but that is not all: "I have inscribed you." Absorb the fullness of this! Everything about you and all that concerns you have I put there. Will you ever say again that your God has forsaken you, since He has inscribed you on His own palms?

Unwelcome Guests

*For the weapons of our warfare are not carnal
but mighty in God for pulling down strongholds,
casting down arguments and every high thing that exalts
itself against the knowledge of God, bringing every
thought into captivity to the obedience of Christ.*
– 2 Corinthians 10:4-5 –

When a thought of anxiety comes knocking on the door of your mind, you must refuse it entrance. If you invite it in, it will have dinner with you, and if it has dinner with you it will quickly move in and want to spend the night.

The Work of My Hands (I)

And let the beauty and delightfulness and favor
of the LORD our God be upon us; confirm and
establish the work of our hands – yes, the work
of our hands, confirm and establish it.
– Psalm 90:17 AMP –

It's a wonderful thing to know that God's favor and blessing can be upon the work we are doing. Sometimes we can mistakenly think that God only cares about the work of the pastors, youth leaders, choir members, and missionaries, but doesn't care about us and what we do.

It is easy to think that a job in the workplace is secular work and a job in the church is Christian work. If God has provided you with a job in the workplace He wants to bless you in the workplace. All honorable work that is done unto the Lord can glorify Him and accomplish His purpose.

The Work of My Hands (II)

God wants to bless the work of your hands. He wants to bless your employer through the work you do. He wants to bless others through the work of your hands, and He wants to bless you. He wants to bless you with success, with an income, with productivity, and with favor.

Lord, thank You for my job and for allowing me to be in the workplace. Thank You that this is Your appointed place for me at this time. Thank You that You care about me and what I do. I am so glad to know that I can have Your blessing upon my life and upon what I do.

Bless the work of my hands today. Bless the company I work for and make them successful. I thank You for the income that I am receiving through this work and that I can use it to meet my needs and bless others. Continue to bless me and grant me Your favor.

Amen.

Punctuation Marks (I)

Are you going through a time of change in your life? How does God want you to view this change? Consider your life like a story that God is writing, one sentence at a time. This time of change is one of the sentences in your story. Sentences are written with punctuation marks, and each punctuation mark has a different meaning. If God were punctuating this time of change in your life what punctuation mark would He use?

God would not use a period. A period would leave you with the sense that you were at the end. This could lead you into despair and discouragement. Your life is not over just because you are going through change, no matter how great that change may be. God promises you hope and a future.

God would not use a question mark. A question mark would leave you with the sense of uncertainty. Uncertainty would be the doorway that leads you into worry. God does not want you to worry about the change you are going through or worry about what is ahead. God has promised to take care of you and He has told you not to be anxious about your life.

Punctuation Marks (II)

"Do not remember the former things, nor consider the things of old. Behold, I will do a new thing, Now it shall spring forth; shall you not know it? I will even make a road in the wilderness and rivers in the desert."
– Isaiah 43:18-19 –

In this time of change, God would not use an exclamation point. An exclamation point would leave you with a sense of high emotion. Exclamations points have been called "screamers" or "gaspers." These are the things that would lead you into panic and fear. God has not given you the spirit of fear, and He has promised to give you His peace.

Since God would not use a period, a question mark, or an exclamation point, which form of punctuation would He use?

God would use a comma. The reason God would use a comma to punctuate a time of change is because a comma means a brief pause. A comma lets you know that the sentence has not come to an end. A comma says that after the brief pause, something else will follow. God wants you to know that there is something ahead that He has planned for you.

May

True Hope

*Paul, an apostle of Jesus Christ by the
commandment of God our Saviour, and
Lord Jesus Christ, which is our hope.*
– 1 Timothy 1:1 KJV –

No man or government has the power to change the greatest enemies that face every generation. It is foolish to put our hope in man. Man has no power to change the human heart, to deliver from sin, to outsmart the devil, to take away the darkness that covers the soul, or to stop the certainty of death.

When Jesus is your future you can set your heart, your thoughts, your faith, and your hope in Him because He cannot fail and He will never change.

Hope in God's Eternal Plan

In Psalm 42:5 (AMP) we read, "Why are you cast down, O my inner self? And why should you moan over me and be disquieted within me? Hope in God and wait expectantly for Him, for I shall yet praise Him, my Help and my God."

The Bible tells us plainly that the world is going in the wrong direction and moving there at a rapid pace. Consider these words from the apostle Paul when he wrote to the church in 1 Corinthians 7:29 (AMP). "I mean, brethren, the appointed time has been winding down and it has grown very short."

The apostle John tells us "And the world is passing away, and the lust of it; but he who does the will of God abides forever" (1 John 2:17).

Jesus told those who would follow Him not to expect things to be easy, but this is not the time for those who know their God to be downcast or gloomy. Jesus is still the King of kings and the Lord of lords. He is at the right hand of the Father and soon He shall descend from heaven with a shout, with the voice of the archangel, and with the trump of God.

Keep Your Heart Full of Hope

*The kingdoms of this world have become
the kingdoms of our Lord and of His Christ,
and He shall reign forever and ever!*
– Revelation 11:15 –

Today, God wants us to keep our hope in Him and not in this world's system or its leaders. Jesus has kept us in the world but we are not of the world. He has us here for an eternal purpose – to be a light of hope that needs to be seen; to be a voice of truth that needs to be heard; to be a demonstration of love that needs to be lived.

Let's never forget that man's plans will fail, but it is God's plan that will prevail. It is His kingdom that is coming; it is His truth that will have the final say in all things. The change that God brings will be everlasting – the world will pass away, sin will be no more, death will be overcome, the devil and all his demons will be cast into hell, Jesus will reign in righteousness, and there will be a new heaven and earth that is flooded by His glorious light. This is our true hope.

"No Sweat" (I)

But the Levitical priests ... they shall enter into My sanctuary; and they shall come near to My table to minister to Me, ... no wool shall be on them while they minister at the gates of the inner court and within the temple. They shall have linen turbans on their heads and linen breeches upon their loins; they shall not gird themselves with anything that causes [them to] sweat.
– Ezekiel 44:15-18 AMP –

One of the amazing things we discover in the Bible is that a single little word can be like a powerful spotlight which reveals to our spiritual eyes a truth of gigantic proportions. The word "sweat" that is used in Ezekiel 44 is one of those words. "Sweat" represents the work, the labor, and the natural efforts of our flesh.

In his devotional book *A Table in the Wilderness*, Watchman Nee points out the following:

The symbolism takes us back, I think, to Genesis 3 and man's fall. Because of it the curse rested on the ground, which therefore ceased to yield fruit without man's effort, and Adam was told: "In the sweat of thy face shalt thou eat bread."

"No Sweat" (II)

In Ezekiel 44, the context of the word "sweat" ties back to the manner in which the priests of the Lord were to minister to Him in the inner court. The inner court was the place of God's presence. It was within the inner court that the glory of the Lord rested upon the mercy seat. It is through the shed blood of Jesus Christ that the way into the presence of the Lord has been opened to us. The work of redemption is Jesus' work alone; our own efforts (sweat) can add nothing to His finished work.

What is true of our redemption is also true of our ministry. Both begin at a place of rest. God does not want us to serve Him out of the energy and efforts of our flesh, but in the power and strength of the Holy Spirit.

"No Sweat" (III)

The apostle Paul tells us, "But by the grace of God I am what I am, and His grace toward me was not in vain; but I labored more abundantly than they all, yet not I, but the grace of God which was with me" (1 Cor. 15:10).

It is clear from this passage that spiritual rest does not mean spiritual passivity. Paul is telling us that his ministry was based on "rest in action" and not "rest from action." Paul understood the meaning of "sweat" spoken of by Ezekiel. Paul served the Lord in the garment of linen (the Holy Spirit) and not in the garment of wool (self-effort.) I believe that is an important lesson for each of us to learn as we serve Him. To minister in the garment of linen means that we minister:

1. To the Lord – drawing close to His heart in fellowship and intimacy.
2. Through the Lord – in the power of His might and the grace He provides.
3. For the Lord – doing all for His glory in a way that pleases Him.

Growth

It is said that a mother found her small boy standing beside a tall sunflower, with his feet stuck in the ground. When she asked, "What are you doing?" he naively answered, "Why, I am trying to grow to be a man."

His mother laughed heartily at the idea of his being planted in the ground in order to grow like the sunflower. Then, patting him gently on the head, she said, "Why, Harry, that is not the way to grow. You can never grow bigger by trying. Just come right in and eat enough good food and have plenty of play and you will soon grow to be a man without trying so hard." Harry's mother was right. There could not be a better answer to the question: "How do the lilies grow?" than Hannah White-hall Smith's comment, "They grow without trying."

We live continually on His life, being nourished, fed and constantly filled with His Spirit and presence and all the fullness of His imparted life.

– A. B. SIMPSON

I Would Rather

I would rather be in the darkness with God
than in the light with thousands.
I would rather be alone with Him
than surrounded by the crowd.

I would rather be under the discipline of my Lord
than to hear the applause of man.
I find more value in leaving all for Jesus Christ
than in seeking the riches of this world.

I would rather hear His sweet voice at sunrise
than to sleep well and miss my appointment with the King.
I would rather invest my time and energy in Jesus
than waste my time on what is not eternal.

My desire is to know Him more
and to be more like Him.
Yes, my Beloved ...
I would rather have You!

– BEVERLY LESSIN

Your Value (I)

Christ died for us.
– Romans 5:8 –

At auctions people bid on items they value. Each item purchased is worth whatever someone is willing to pay – the greater the value, the greater the price. One of the things that will increase the value of an item is its rarity. If there are 100 of an item it has some value, if there are only ten of that same item it has greater value, but if there is only one of that item in existence it has the greatest value of all.

Have you ever wondered what your true value is? If your life were up for auction what would you be worth? When Jesus went to the cross He paid the highest price that could ever be paid for your life. To God you are worth the death of His Son. Why such a high price? There are not 100 of you, there are not ten of you, there is only one of you. If you are lost someone cannot be your replacement. That is why Jesus came to seek and to save you. He was not willing that you should perish. You are the lost sheep that needed to be found.

Your Value (II)

There were ninety and nine that safely lay
In the shelter of the fold;
But one was out on the hills away,
Far off from the gates of gold.
Away on the mountains wild and bare;
Away from the tender Shepherd's care.
"Lord, Thou hast here Thy ninety and nine;
Are they not enough for Thee?"
But the Shepherd made answer: "This of Mine
Has wandered away from Me.
And although the road be rough and steep,
I go to the desert to find My sheep."
But none of the ransomed ever knew
How deep were the waters crossed;
Nor how dark was the night the Lord passed through
Ere He found His sheep that was lost.
"Lord, whence are Thy hands so rent and torn?"
"They're pierced tonight by many a thorn."
And all through the mountains, thunder-riv'n,
And up from the rocky steep,
There arose a glad cry to the gate of heav'n,
"Rejoice! I have found My sheep!"
And the angels echoed around the throne,
"Rejoice, for the Lord brings back His own!"

– ELIZABETH C. CLEPHANE

His Abundant and Glorious Work

The rain of His grace is always dropping; the river of His bounty is ever flowing; the well-spring of His love is constantly over-flowing. Daily His branches bend down to our hand with a fresh store of mercy. Who can know the number of His benefits or recount the list of His bounties? The countless stars are like the standard bearers of a more innumerable host of blessings. Oh, that my praise would be as ceaseless as His bounty!

– CHARLES H. SPURGEON

God has foreordained the works to which He has called you. He has been ahead of you preparing the place to which you are coming and manipulating all the resources of the universe in order that the work you do may be a part of His whole great and gracious work.

– G. CAMPBELL MORGAN

Jesus Makes All the Difference

Let it be known to you all, and to all the people
of Israel, that by the name of Jesus Christ of Nazareth,
whom you crucified, whom God raised from
the dead, by Him this man stands here before
you whole. This is the "stone which was rejected
by you builders, which has become the chief
cornerstone" Nor is there salvation in any other,
for there is no other name under heaven given
among men by which we must be saved.

– Acts 4:10-12 –

Live in the peace of knowing that God has accepted you.

Live in the confidence of knowing that Christ's blood makes you clean.

Live in the joy of knowing you are forgiven.

Live in the assurance of knowing that He is holding your hand.

Live in the hope of knowing that your future is secure with Jesus.

Jesus Is ...

Because He is your Lord, worship Him.
- Psalm 45:11 -

His majesty is your worship,
His holiness is your beauty,
His presence is your fragrance,
His truth is your foundation,
His tenderness is your comfort,
His abundance is your supply,
His plan is your purpose,
His faithfulness is your security,
His life is your fulfillment,
His strength is your endurance,
His heart is your home.

Looking Up; Looking Down (I)

"Keep looking down!" this statement is a proclamation of a believer's position in Christ. It is based upon Ephesians 2:6, "For He raised us from the dead along with Christ and seated us with Him in the heavenly realms because we are united with Christ Jesus."

Some think that the saying, "keep looking down" is a negative statement, while the phrase "keeping looking up" is a positive one. The truth is that both statements are positive when viewed from a proper perspective.

We are told in Hebrews 12:1-2, "Let us run with patience the race that is set before us, looking unto Jesus the author and finisher of our faith." God does want us to keep an upward view, keeping our eyes on Jesus as we daily serve Him and follow Him with all of our hearts.

It is important for us to "keep looking up." It is our upward look that keeps hope in our hearts and Christ's coming kingdom before us. "Looking up" means that we are not hanging our heads in discouragement and being weighed down with despair. "Looking up" keeps us moving forward, from faith to faith and glory to glory.

Looking Up; Looking Down (II)

As important as it is for us to daily be "looking up" it is equally important for us to be daily "looking down." Through our spiritual eyes God has allowed us to have these two distinctive views of faith. You can "keep looking up" because you are on a pilgrim's journey here on earth. You can keep "looking down" because you are seated with Christ in heavenly places.

What does the perspective of "keep looking down" mean in your daily walk? It means that you are seated with Christ in a place of rest, in a place of triumph, in a place of power, in a place of authority, and in a place of glory. His place is your place; His victory is your victory; His life is your life. You can "keep looking down" because He has conquered the grave, because the enemy is below His feet, and because you are more than a conqueror through Him who loves you.

Comfort

All praise to God, the Father of our
Lord Jesus Christ. God is our merciful
Father and the source of all comfort.
He comforts us in all our troubles.
– 2 Corinthians 1:3-4 NLT –

God's comfort is truly an amazing thing. Think about the image of a mother coming to the aid of her frightened child. The immediate response of the mother is to bring her child comfort. How does she do it? She brings comfort by reaching out and picking up her crying child in her arms. Once her child is secure in her arms, she draws her child close to her heart. As she does, she begins to speak soft, soothing words to reassure her child that she is near and all will be well once again.

Like that child, we all have need of God's comfort. Have you felt His arms lift you and draw you close to His heart? Have you heard His voice saying, "Peace, be still."

The Adventure of Obedience

God can do anything He wants to do, at any time He wants –
if we are yielded to Him. Life is never boring when we are walking in obedience to the Lord.

– BEVERLY LESSIN

Listen carefully to everything He tells you.
– Acts 3:22 NLT –

"Whatever He says to you, do it."
– John 2:5 –

The Scripture from John 2:5 is part of a devotional reading for May 11 from the book, *Thoughts for the Quiet
Hour* by Dwight L. Moody. The devotional continues
with the following words from Florence Nightingale:

If I could give you information of my life, it would
be to show how a woman of very ordinary ability has
been led by God in strange and unaccustomed paths
to do in His service what He has done in her. And if
I could tell you all, you would see how God has done
all, and I nothing. I have worked hard, very hard,
that is all; and I have never refused God anything.

What God Has Done for You

Consider what great things He has done for you.

– 1 SAMUEL 12:24

Look back on all the way the Lord your God has led you. Do you not see it dotted with ten thousand blessings in disguise? Call to mind the needed Succor sent at the critical moment; the right way chosen for you instead of the wrong way you had chosen for yourself; the hurtful thing to which your heart so fondly clung, removed out of your path; the breathing-time granted, which your tried and struggling spirit just at the moment needed. Oh, has not Jesus stood at your side when you knew it not? Has not Infinite Love encircled every cloud with its merciful lining? Oh, retrace your steps, and mark His footprint in each one! Thank Him for them all, and learn the needed lesson of leaning more simply on Jesus.

– F. WHITFIELD

God is over all things, under all things, outside all things; within, but not enclosed; without, but not excluded; above, but not raised up; below, but not depressed; wholly above presiding, wholly beneath sustaining, wholly without embracing, and wholly within filling.

– ANONYMOUS

Abba Father

*You received the Spirit of adoption by
whom we cry out, "Abba, Father."*
– Romans 8:15 –

What is the loudest sound that you hear within you? What is the sound that rings the loudest day in and day out? Have you been quiet enough in your inner man to know? The loudest sounds that you hear and listen to are the true indicators of what is really happening in your spiritual walk. What you do and the choices you make are by-products of what is going on within you.

What sound rings the loudest in the very center of your being? Is it Jesus? Is it "Abba, Father"? Can you really say, whatever your age, whatever your circumstance, that apart from all the good and beautiful sounds that you hear within you, Jesus' voice rings loudest. When anything else becomes the center of your being, when work or ministry, husband or wife, or son or daughter becomes the center of your being, then it is time to re-examine your heart's deepest priorities and affections. At school, at work, at play, the sound that rings the loudest within you should be Abba, Abba, Abba, Abba, Father – that's who I live for!

– DON LESSIN, *ABBA CRY*

Majesty

A writer, Trieste Van Wyngarden, was on a flight from Northern California to Dallas, Texas. As the plane flew over Arizona she heard the pilot announce, "For those of you on the left side of the plane, you will soon be seeing a spectacular view of the Grand canyon." She was thankful she was seated in a window seat. It was her first view of the canyon. As she gazed in wonder at the beauty that passed before her eyes she found her heart declaring, "The Lord has carved His name on the earth ... it is Majesty."

There are certain words that are only fitting for God to claim. Majesty is one of them. Majesty is a proclamation of His greatness, His grandeur, His splendor and His magnificence. God's majesty leaves us in awe of who He is and what He does. God is the "awe" in "awesome", the "wonder" in "wondrous", the "splendid" in "splendor", the "magnificent" in "magnificence", and the "grand" in "grandeur". No one else and nothing else can measure up to His greatness.

God's Majesty

To the one only God, our Savior through Jesus Christ our Lord, be glory (splendor), majesty, might and dominion, and power and authority, before all time and now and forever (unto all the ages of eternity). Amen (so be it).
– Jude 1:25 AMP –

God is the Majesty on High (Heb. 1).

God is clothed with majesty (Ps. 93).

His voice is full of majesty (Ps. 29).

Majesty is found in His presence (1 Chron. 16).

His majesty is over His people (Ps. 68).

Majesty is before Him (Ps. 96).

His majesty is filled with glorious splendor (Ps. 145).

His majesty leads us into worship (Isa. 24).

His majesty covers all the earth! (Ps. 8).

The Heart of God Revealed (I)

In the eleventh chapter of Hosea, as God laments over His people's waywardness, we gain a marvelous insight into the heart of God. In verse four we read, "I drew them with gentle cords, with bands of love, and I was to them as those who take the yoke from their neck. I stooped and fed them."

I drew them ... Even when we are trying to pull away from God, He is drawing us back to Himself. God's heart does not push us away, ignore us, or block us from coming to Him. There is a cord of grace and kindness that is extended to us, a lifeline to His heart. God's desire for us is to be with Him, to know Him, and to be cared for by Him.

The Heart of God Revealed (II)

With gentle cords ... God doesn't yank the cord He uses to draw us to Himself. He is patient with us. He waits for us to respond to His gentle tug upon our hearts. His does not attempt to overpower us – He comes to us meekly, peaceably and full of mercy.

> *Now I, Paul, myself am pleading with you*
> *by the meekness and gentleness of Christ.*
> *– 2 Corinthians 10:1 –*

> *He is able to exercise gentleness and*
> *forbearance toward the ignorant and erring.*
> *– Hebrews 5:2 AMP –*

The Heart of God Revealed (III)

With bands of love ... The bands of God that He places around us are not made of rope to burn us, or iron to bruise us, or thorns to cut us; they are bands of love to keep us, to restore us, and to heal us. He tenderly longs to hold us as a mother holds her needy child close to her.

> *"Can a woman forget her nursing child,*
> *And not have compassion on the son of her womb?*
> *Surely they may forget, yet I will not forget you.*
> *See, I have inscribed you on the palms of My hands."*
> *– Isaiah 49:15 –*

> *The LORD has appeared of old to me, saying:*
> *"Yes, I have loved you with an everlasting love;*
> *therefore with lovingkindness I have drawn you."*
> *– Jeremiah 31:3 –*

The Heart of God Revealed (IV)

*"Come to Me, all you who labor and are
heavy laden, and I will give you rest. Take My
yoke upon you and learn from Me, for I am gentle and
lowly in heart, and you will find rest for your souls.
For My yoke is easy and My burden is light."*
– Matthew 11:28-29 –

I took the yoke from their neck ... The heart of God wants to free us, not bind us. There is no freedom for us until His power releases us from all bondage, fear, and enslavement of sin. His Father's heart could never leave us helplessly yoked to any enemy of His love.

The Heart of God Revealed (V)

The LORD is my shepherd; I shall not want.
He makes me to lie down in green pastures; He leads
me beside the still waters. He restores my soul; He leads
me in the paths of righteousness For His name's sake.
Yea, though I walk through the valley of the shadow of
death, I will fear no evil; for You are with me; Your rod
and Your staff, they comfort me. You prepare a table
before me in the presence of my enemies; You anoint my
head with oil; my cup runs over. Surely goodness and
mercy shall follow me all the days of my life; and
I will dwell in the house of the LORD forever.
– Psalm 23:1-6 –

I stooped and fed them ... What a picture of the heart of God – the Almighty, the Creator, the One who is above all and over all, bends down to us like a father bends down to pick up a crying child. He bends down so we can see His tender look, His caring expression, and His soft smile. Then, as we find comfort and assurance, He lifts us – to meet our needs, to calm our fears, and to draw us ever nearer to His heart.

Eyes to See the Unexpected (I)

Now faith is the substance of things hoped for,
the evidence of things not seen.
– Hebrews 11:1 KJV –

When the disciples were faced with the need of feeding thousands of people who were hungry, they took inventory of their circumstances and concluded they were in an impossible situation. In their thinking, there were too many empty stomachs for the amount of food on hand. Their solution was a pragmatic one, "send them all away and let them find their own food."

When Jesus told them to feed the crowd they quickly replied, "With what?" "What's available?" Jesus asked them. Through their eyes they could only see a tiny snack made up of a few fish and a couple of loaves of bread, but through Jesus' eyes, He could see a feast in the making. Jesus took something that was right in front of their eyes and did the unexpected. By blessing the fish and breaking the bread He multiplied what was available and used it to feed a multitude.

Eyes to See the Unexpected (II)

The book of Second Kings tells the account of a widow who was in a desperate situation. She had no money and faced losing her two sons, who were about to be taken as slaves by a creditor. When the prophet Elisha asked her what she had of value in the house the widow said, "Nothing really, just a small jar of oil." Through her eyes the oil didn't amount to much, but through Elisha's eyes the oil amounted to a treasure chest of wealth. The widow never expected God to use her little jar of oil to bring about her deliverance as she obediently poured it from vessel to vessel.

When Moses asked God how he could convince Israel that the Lord had sent him, God answered, "What is in your hand?" Moses answered, "A rod." Moses must have thought, "How can this lifeless thing convince anybody that God has sent me to lead His people out of Egypt?" Moses didn't think he held anything in his hand that God would use to reveal His glory and power in delivering a nation.

Are you facing something that looks impossible? Do you need to see God move in a mighty way? Don't be surprised if His answer comes in a way that is unexpected and that He uses something that is already in your hand, or right under your nose.

Eyes to See the Unexpected (III)

But their eyes were prevented from recognizing Him.
– Luke 24:16 –

And their eyes were opened and they recognized Him.
– Luke 24:31 –

There is much precious significance in this. The Lord is often present in our lives in things that we do not dream possess any significance. We are asking God about something which needs His mighty working, and the very instrument by which He is to work is by our side, perhaps for weeks and months and years all unrecognized, until suddenly someday it grows luminous and glorious with the very presence of the Lord, and becomes the mighty instrument of His hand through the unexpected. Often He keeps us from seeing His way until just before He opens it, and then, immediately that it is unfolded, we find that He was walking by our side in the very thing, long before we even suspected its meaning.

– A. B. SIMPSON

The Lesson of Lilies and Birds

*"That is why I tell you not to worry about
everyday life – whether you have enough
food and drink, or enough clothes to wear.
Isn't life more than food, and your body more than
clothing? Look at the birds. They don't plant or
harvest or store food in barns, for your heavenly
Father feeds them. And aren't you far more valuable
to Him than they are? Can all your worries add
a single moment to your life? And why worry
about your clothing? Look at the lilies of the field
and how they grow. They don't work or make their
clothing, yet Solomon in all his glory was not
dressed as beautifully as they are. And if God cares
so wonderfully for wildflowers that are here today
and thrown into the fire tomorrow, He will certainly
care for you. Why do you have so little faith?"*
– Matthew 6:25-30 NLT –

If you ever see a lily toiling or a bird storing up food in
a barn, then you will know that the time to worry has
arrived.

Trust

Never be afraid to trust an unknown future to a known God.

– CORRIE TEN BOOM

When a train goes through a tunnel and it gets dark, you don't throw away the ticket and jump off. You sit still and trust the engineer.

– CORRIE TEN BOOM

So do not throw away this confident trust in the Lord. Remember the great reward it brings you! Patient endurance is what you need now, so that you will continue to do God's will. Then you will receive all that He has promised.

– HEBREWS 10:35-36 NLT

June

Real Grace for Real People (I)

The grace of our Lord Jesus Christ be with you.
– 2 Thessalonians 3:18 KJV –

A famous quote by Shakespeare begins with these words, "All the world's a stage, and all the men and women merely players." For many people, life is nothing more than playing out a role. They "act" their way through life, trying to gain the approval and acceptance of others. They are bound by the fear of being exposed for who they really are, and so they perform, playing out a role in order to receive applause and recognition. Many Christians live this way, trying to impress others by acting out a spiritual role.

The life of Jesus brings us into reality, not role playing. In order to live in His reality we must first be real with Him. He wants us to come to Him as we are. He knows everything about us. We do not need to try and impress Him or win Him over with a good performance. We must come to Him in sincerity and truth, in humility and brokenness, and in openness and honesty. When we come to Him in this way, He will not cast us out. He does not meet us with judgment but with mercy; He does not extend condemnation but grace.

Real Grace for Real People (II)

He gives more grace. Therefore He says: "God resists the proud, But gives grace to the humble." Therefore submit to God. Resist the devil and he will flee from you. Draw near to God and He will draw near to you.

– James 4:6-8 KJV –

Grace is one of the most freeing things we can ever receive and experience in life. Grace justifies you and brings you His salvation (Titus 2:11, 3:7.)

Grace means that God has accepted you and received you into His family as His child, not because of your good performance, but because of what Jesus Christ has done for you. Grace means that God freely gives you what you don't deserve.

Real Grace for Real People (III)

God has not called us to role playing, but to reality living based upon His grace.

A role is earned. Grace is given.
    A role is performed. Grace is received.
A role produces effort. Grace produces rest.
    A role says "do." Grace says "be."
A role is labor. Grace is a flow.
    A role depletes. Grace energizes.
A role demands. Grace releases.
    A role produces results. Grace produces fruit.
A role brings praise to man. Grace brings praise to God.

Are you in need? There's no point in "acting" like everything is great, instead, go to God in prayer and receive His grace.

Real Grace for Real People (IV)

Let us therefore come boldly unto the
throne of grace, that we may obtain mercy,
and find grace to help in time of need.
– Hebrews 4:16 KJV –

Do you sense your weakness? There's no need to grit your teeth and bear it with a painted smile, instead receive the strength that God gives you through His grace.

Be strong in the grace that is in Christ Jesus.
– 2 Timothy 2:1 KJV –

Are you discouraged? There's no need to try and "keep your chin up", instead, draw upon the comfort and wonderful hope that comes to you through His grace.

Real Grace for Real People (V)

Now may our Lord Jesus Christ Himself and God our Father, who loved us and by His grace gave us eternal comfort and a wonderful hope, comfort you and strengthen you in every good thing you do and say.
– 2 Thessalonians 2:16-17 NLT –

Do you want to live a life that is pleasing to Him? There's no need to strive and try to make things happen, instead, walk in the grace that enables you to glorify Him.

That the name of our Lord Jesus Christ may be glorified in you, and you in Him, according to the grace of our God and the Lord Jesus Christ.
– 2 Thessalonians 1:12 NKJV –

Do you feel blue? There's no need to "whistle a happy tune", instead, let the grace of God put a new song in your heart.

Let the word of Christ dwell in you richly in all wisdom; singing with grace in your hearts to the Lord.
– Colossians 3:16 KJV –

Waiting

God doesn't always answer our prayers at the moment we ask. It may be His plan to answer us, but not always in the timetable we think. Also, God doesn't always fulfill the words He speaks to us at the moment He reveals them. Why does God sometimes delay and what does He want us to learn while we are waiting.

The book of Hebrews gives us some wonderful insight into this question, "We desire that each one of you show the same diligence to the full assurance of hope until the end, that you do not become sluggish, but imitate those who through faith and patience inherit the promises (Heb. 6:11-12 NKJV).

Here, in paraphrase form, is God's answer to the question of waiting, "In times of waiting I want you to learn to stay steady and attentive to what I am saying. I want you to develop a hope that will keep you moving forward in my will until the end of your journey. Above all, I want you to add to your faith the benefit of patience, which will allow you to wait without complaint and with a calm willingness to receive what I have for you, in the time frame that fits perfectly into My plan for your life."

The 10 Greatest Powers
in the Universe (I)

1. **The Power of the Gospel:** nothing else can save your soul. *For I am not ashamed of the gospel of Christ, for it is the power of God to salvation for everyone who believes, for the Jew first and also for the Greek (Rom. 1:16).*

2. **The Power of the Blood of Jesus:** nothing else can cleanse you from sin. *But if we walk in the light as He is in the light, we have fellowship with one another, and the blood of Jesus Christ His Son cleanses us from all sin (1 John 1:7).*

3. **The Power of the Cross:** nothing else can deliver you from yourself. *Knowing this, that our old man was crucified with Him, that the body of sin might be done away with, that we should no longer be slaves of sin (Rom. 6:6).*

4. **The Power of the Word:** nothing else can bring you transforming truth. *Sanctify them by Your truth. Your word is truth (John 17:17).*

5. **The Power of God:** nothing else can keep you from evil. *And do not lead us into temptation, but deliver us from the evil one. For Yours is the kingdom and the power and the glory forever. Amen (Matt. 6:13).*

The 10 Greatest Powers
in the Universe (II)

6. **The Power of the Holy Spirit:** nothing else can make you like Jesus. *But we all, with unveiled face, beholding as in a mirror the glory of the Lord, are being transformed into the same image from glory to glory, just as by the Spirit of the Lord (2 Cor. 3:18).*

7. **The Power of the Resurrection:** nothing else can give you eternal hope. *Blessed be the God and Father of our Lord Jesus Christ, who according to His abundant mercy has begotten us again to a living hope through the resurrection of Jesus Christ from the dead (1 Pet. 1:3).*

8. **The Power of Prayer:** nothing else can move the hand of God. *"And whatever things you ask in prayer, believing, you will receive" (Matt. 21:22)*

9. **The Power of Grace:** nothing else can make you completely sufficient. *God is able to make all grace abound toward you, that you, always having all sufficiency in all things, may have an abundance for every good work (2 Cor. 9:8).*

10. **The Power of Faith:** nothing else can keep you till the end. *Who are kept by the power of God through faith for salvation ready to be revealed in the last time (1 Pet. 1:5).*

Tranquility

God is tranquil. So must your spirit become a tranquil and clear little pool, wherein the serene light of God can be mirrored. Therefore shun all that is disquieting and distracting, both within and without. Nothing in the whole world is worth the loss of your peace; even the faults which you have committed should only humble, but not disquiet, you. God is full of joy, peace, and happiness. Endeavor then to obtain a continually joyful and peaceful spirit. Avoid all anxious care, vexation, murmuring, and melancholy, which darken your soul and render you unfit for the friendship of God. If you perceive such feelings arising, turn gently away from them.

– GERHARD TERSTEEGEN

Worry does not empty tomorrow of its sorrow. It empties today of its strength.

– CORRIE TEN BOOM

Abide in Peace

"Let be and be still, and know (recognize and understand) that I am God."

– PSALM 46:10 AMP

The crosses which we make for ourselves by a restless anxiety as to the future, are not crosses which come from God. We show want of faith in Him by our false wisdom wishing to forestall His arrangements, and struggling to supplement His providence by our own providence.

The future is not yet ours; perhaps it never will be. If it comes, it may come wholly different from what we have foreseen. Let us shut our eyes, then, to that which God hides from us and keeps in reserve in the treasure of His deep counsels. Let us worship without seeing; let us be silent; let us abide in peace.

– FRANÇOIS FENÉLON

Jesus, Our Only Option (I)

Even though we like variety and are thankful for all the options that present themselves to us in life, there are times when the options before us bring frustration and confusion. Clearly some choices are much more important than others. It is one thing to decide which box of cereal to eat; it is quite another thing to decide which college to attend, which career to pursue, or which person to marry.

Thankfully, when it comes to the most important decision in life, God has made it very simple for us. He does not present to us a "supermarket" of spiritual paths that we may choose in order to know and follow Him. He does not say to us, "Go down this aisle and look over all the spiritual options I have given you and then pick the one that suits you best."

Our decision to know and follow God is so important that He has presented us with only one option. Every road sign God has made points to one person; every message God has spoken proclaims one name; every view God shows us of Himself reveals one face.

At this moment, for you, Jesus Christ is God's only option.

Jesus, Our Only Option (II)

Jesus is the message of all God wants to say to you.
Then a cloud overshadowed them, and a voice from the cloud said, "This is my dearly loved Son. Listen to Him" (Mark 9:7).

He is the image of all God wants to show to you.
He is the image of the invisible God (Col. 1:15).

He is the fullness of all God wants to give to you.
For it has pleased [the Father] that all the divine fullness (the sum total of the divine perfection, powers, and attributes) should dwell in Him permanently (Col. 1:19 AMP).

He is the essence of all God wants to be to you.
Blessed be the God and Father of our Lord Jesus Christ, who has blessed us with every spiritual blessing in the heavenly places in Christ, just as He chose us in Him before the foundation of the world (Eph. 1:3-4).

Jesus, Our Only Option (III)

Yet for us there is one God, the Father, of whom are all things, and we for Him; and one Lord Jesus Christ, through whom are all things, and through whom we live.
– 1 Corinthians 8:6 –

That in the dispensation of the fullness of the times He might gather together in one all things in Christ, both which are in heaven and which are on earth – in Him.
– Ephesians 1:10 –

From God's point of view, Jesus is not a good option or the best option, but the only option He has given us. Without Jesus we have nothing and we can do nothing, yet with Him we have all things. All that is in God's heart for us is found in Jesus Christ.

The best thing anyone can do and the best decision anyone can make is to give all to Jesus Christ. It is as we give our all, for His all, that we find all we were made to be. God would never ask to look anywhere else, because if He did, He would be leading us astray.

Jesus, Our Only Option (IV)

To have God's all in Jesus we must begin by giving Him our all. C. S. Lewis reminds us:

> For it is not so much of our time and so much of our attention that God demands; it is not even all our time and all our attention; it is ourselves. He has, in the last resort, nothing to give us but Himself; and He can give that only insofar as our self-affirming will retires and makes room for Him in our souls. Let us make up our minds to it; there will be nothing "of our own" left over to live on, no "ordinary" life. What cannot be allowed is the idea of something that is "our own" some area in which we are to be "out of school" on which God has no claim. For He claims all, because He is love and must bless. He cannot bless us unless He has us. When we try to keep within us an area that is our own, we try to keep an area of death. Therefore, in love, He claims all. There's no bargaining with Him.

Jesus Our Only Option (V)

Consider this prayer today as you lay all at His feet:

Jesus, I choose to be wholly Yours;

thank You that You have come

to be wholly mine.

I lose my life in Your life;

I put my faith in Your faithfulness;

I find my song in Your joy.

You are my portion forever, my hope,

my purpose, my life.

Thank You that You are my only glorious,

wondrous, marvelous option!

I embrace You with all my heart,

I follow You with all my will, I worship

You with all my adoration.

Amen.

Jesus, Our Only Option (VI)

Although it has only three letters, the word "all" has huge implications. "All" means total, complete, or whole. In a baseball game, if one team scored all the runs it means the other team scored none.

If one candidate received all the votes in an election it means the other candidate received none.

If a doctor tells you to take all of your antibiotics it means he doesn't want any left over.

The word "all" is another way God affirms to us who Jesus, His Son, truly is. If Jesus is the "all" of God, it means that God has eliminated every other option.

Jesus, Our Only Option (VII)

Here are a few of the "alls" that we find in Scripture concerning Jesus Christ:

All things were created by Jesus
All things were made by Him; and without Him was not anything made that was made (John 1:3).

All things were created for Jesus
All things were created through Him and for Him (Col. 1:16).

All things hold together in Jesus
And He is before all things, and in Him all things consist (Col. 1:17).

All things are subservient to Jesus
And He is the head of the body, the church, that in all things He may have the preeminence (Col. 1:18).

All things are reconciled by Jesus
By Him to reconcile all things to Himself, by Him, whether things on earth or things in heaven, having made peace through the blood of His cross (Col. 1:20).

Jesus Our Only Option (VIII)

All things are through Jesus
Yet for us there is one God, the Father, of whom are all things, and we for Him; and one Lord Jesus Christ, through whom are all things, and through whom we live (1 Cor. 8:6).

All things belong to Jesus
All things that the Father has are Mine (John 16:15).

All things are under the authority of Jesus
Of whom are the fathers and from whom, according to the flesh, Christ came, who is over all, the eternally blessed God. Amen (Rom. 9:5).

All things will be gathered together in Jesus
That in the dispensation of the fullness of the times He might gather together in one all things in Christ, both which are in heaven and which are on earth – in Him (Eph. 1:10).

All blessings are provided in Jesus
Blessed be the God and Father of our Lord Jesus Christ, who hath blessed us with all spiritual blessings in heavenly places in Christ (Eph. 1:3).

Jesus Our Only Option (IX)

All victory is secured in Jesus
Which He wrought in Christ, when He raised Him from the dead, and set Him at His own right hand in the heavenly places, far above all principality, and power, and might, and dominion, and every name that is named, not only in this world, but also in that which is to come (Eph. 1:21).

All dominion belongs to Jesus
And hath put all things under His feet, and gave Him to be the head over all things to the church (Eph. 1:22).

All fullness is found in Jesus
Which is His body, the fullness of Him that filleth all in all (Eph. 1:23).

All wisdom and knowledge are in Jesus
Christ, in whom are hidden all the treasures of wisdom and knowledge (Col. 2:3).

All and all is in Jesus
Christ is all, and in all (Col. 3:11).

Jesus, Our Only Option (X)

Christ is all, and in all.
– Colossians 3:11 –

Christ is all – all joy, all peace, all love;
    all grace, all mercy, all goodness;
all might, all splendor, all majesty;
    all truth, all light, all glory;
all hope, all redemption, all salvation;
    all fulfillment, all value, all worth;
all completeness, all wholeness, all oneness;
    all holiness, all beauty, all life.

Christ is in all – in my mind, my will, my heart;
    my praying, my doing, my planning;
my tears, my joys, my contentment;
    my going, my coming, my resting;
my tests, my trials, my difficulties;
    my work, my service, my leisure;
my mountains, my valleys, my pathway.

Jesus, Our Only Option (XI)

Jesus is the way to God. He is the truth about God, and apart from the life He gives, we will never share or know the life of God. So there is no knowledge of God apart from Him.

– DR. MARTYN LLOYD-JONES

The service of Christ is the business of my life. The will of Christ is the law of my life. The presence of Christ is the joy of my life. The glory of Christ is the crown of my life.

– ANONYMOUS

The name of Jesus is the sum total of all delights. It is the music with which the bells of heaven ring; a song in a word; a matchless oratorio in two syllables; a gathering up of the hallelujahs of eternity in five letters.

– CHARLES H. SPURGEON

Jesus, Our Only Option (XII)

When Jesus is your only option it also means:

The Scriptures are yours, because they testify of Him and tell His story. The Father is yours, because He has revealed Himself to you through His Son. The Holy Spirit is yours, because He has been sent to bring you the life of Jesus.

The Body of Christ is yours, because He blesses you through His people. Heaven's Angels are yours, because He is the Captain of the heavenly host.

Ministry is yours, because He has sent you into all the world to make Him known. Prayer is yours, because He has given you access to the throne of God.

Forgiveness is yours, because His blood is upon the mercy seat. Purity is yours, because He is your sanctification.

Righteousness is yours, because you are made the righteousness of God in Him. Liberty is yours, because He has set you free from the power of sin.

Victory is yours, because He has defeated the powers of darkness. Joy is yours, because He has put a new song in your heart.

Jesus, Our Only Option (XIII)

For all things are yours: whether Paul or Apollos
or Cephas, or the world or life or death, or things
present or things to come – all are yours.
And you are Christ's, and Christ is God's.
– 1 Corinthians 3:21-23 –

When Jesus is your only option it also means:

Rest is yours, because He has placed His yoke upon you. Peace is yours, because He has freed you from all condemnation.

Endurance is yours, because His joy is your strength. Comfort is your yours, because His tender mercies cover you.

Purpose is yours, because He guides you according to His will. Love is yours, because your heart has been joined with His.

Covenant is yours, because He claims you as His bride. Hope is yours, because He is your future.

Heaven is yours, because He has gone to prepare a place for you.

When Jesus is your only option, all things are yours, for Jesus is all and in all.

Jesus, Our Only Option (XIV)

Christ who is our life.
– Colossians 3:4–

Jesus is our only option in death and in life; in sorrow and in joy; in disappointment and in delight; in testing and in triumph; in loss and in gain; in grief and in comfort; in battles and in victories won.

In Jesus we find the answers to life's greatest questions: How do we:

- Function in the day to day? By the life of Jesus.
- Know what to believe? By the truth of Jesus.
- Experience comfort? By the compassion of Jesus.
- Have strength to face life's heartaches? By the tenderness of Jesus.
- Overcome hardship? By the faithfulness of Jesus.
- Make the right choices? By the wisdom of Jesus.
- Live free from worry and anxiety? By the peace of Jesus.
- See the enemy defeated? By the victory of Jesus.
- Walk in consistency? By the power of Jesus.
- Care about your neighbor? By the love of Jesus.
- Not carry a cloud of guilt? By the forgiveness of Jesus.

Jesus Our Only Option (XV)

How do we:

- Know rest? By the yoke of Jesus.
- Have purpose? By the call of Jesus.
- Live with hope? By the resurrection of Jesus.
- Function without timidity? By the authority of Jesus.
- Stand free of condemnation? By the intercession of Jesus.
- Keep free from bitterness and resentment? By the mercies of Jesus.
- Follow His will? By the grace of Jesus.
- Find guidance? By the voice of Jesus.
- Know we are loved? By the sacrifice of Jesus.
- Know God's heart? By the fellowship of Jesus.
- Be enriched? By the blessings of Jesus.
- Have strength? By the joy of Jesus.
- Feel secure? By the covering of Jesus.
- Stay focused? By the return of Jesus.

Jesus, Our Only Option (XVI)

Jesus is God's plan "A". Because plan "A" is perfect and complete, there is no need for a plan "B". God has no backup plan for your life. He doesn't need one. God never says to us, "If Jesus, My Son, doesn't work for you, let's try something else."

Any plan "B" is our plan, which comes from our own thinking and rationale. God tells us not to lean upon our own understanding, but to acknowledge Him, the Lord, in every decision as the director of our steps.

Here are two quotes from men of God who understood what it meant to have Jesus as their only option:

God designed us to run on Himself. He Himself is the fuel our spirits were designed to feed on. There is no other. That is why it is just no good asking God to make us happy in our own way ... God cannot give us a happiness and peace apart from Himself, because it is not there. There is no such thing.

– C. S. LEWIS

In Jesus all needful things are laid up for you.

– CHARLES H. SPURGEON

Jesus, Our Only Option (XVII)

For I determined not to know anything among
you except Jesus Christ and Him crucified.
– 1 Corinthians 2:2 NKJV –

Some people think of Jesus as an option. They want Him to only be "present" in their lives. Others think of Jesus as the best option. They want Him to be "prominent" in their lives. God wants Jesus to be the only option in our lives. He is to be "preeminent" in all things.

Jesus must not mean "something" to us, or mean "a lot" to us, but He is to mean everything to us. When He is, we will understand what it means to have Him as our only option.

Jesus, Our Only Option (XVIII)

During World War Two, Corrie ten Boom and her family were taken from their home and placed in a Nazi concentration camp. She miraculously survived the horrors of the camp, but suffered the loss of her entire family. Later on, as she looked back over those dark days in her life, she was able to say, "I know that with Jesus the worst can happen, the best still remains, and His light is stronger than the deepest darkness." She could say this because Jesus was her life, and she had learned through the most difficult experiences of life, that nothing and no one could take from her what mattered most.

As the enjoying of Christ is the enjoying of all, so the loss of Christ is the loss of all.

– RICHARD BAXTER

Jesus, Our Only Option (XIX)

Investment firms tell you it is best to diversify. We are often warned about the danger of putting "all our eggs in one basket." That may be good advice for investing, but when it comes to the subject of your life, the Bible tells us something very different.

God does not tell us to diversify our faith, but He does tell us to "put all our eggs in one basket." God has only one Begotten Son, but He has provided only one way for us to be saved and come into a personal relationship with Him. The only way we can ever receive any spiritual blessing from God is through Jesus Christ.

Having Jesus as your only option would be a bad decision if Jesus stumbled and fell – it would mean that if He fails, you fail; if He loses, you are lost; if He cannot bless you, you are empty; if He is not triumphant, you are defeated; if He is not in control, you are in great danger.

When Jesus is your only option you don't need to say "I'm His, sink or swim," because He will not sink; "I'm His, win or lose," because He will not lose.

Jesus, Our Only Option (XX)

The hard heart receives nothing; the stony heart endures for a season; the cluttered heart gets choked off. It is only the fully surrendered heart that bears fruit that will remain.

In the book of Ruth we are told that Ruth followed Naomi wholeheartedly. Orpah, Naomi's other daughter-in-law, gave herself to Naomi for a season and followed her for a distance before turning back. When Orpah made her choice to turn back, Ruth said to Naomi, "Entreat me not to leave you, or to turn back from following after you" (Ruth 1:16).

The Bible tells us that King Amaziah had something in common with Orpah.

We are told that "he did not serve with a whole heart." King Amaziah was a "nice guy" but his half-heartedness displeased the Lord and caused King Amaziah to make poor decisions that led to his ruin and defeat.

God has made it clear. His Son, Jesus Christ, is our only option. He asks us to give our hearts to no one else, to believe in no one else, to listen to no one else, and to follow no one else. Is Jesus your only option?

July

Two Baskets (I)

For we are God's workmanship, created
in Christ Jesus to do good works, which
God prepared in advance for us to do.
– Ephesians 2:10 NIV –

Did you know that God has put good things within you that He wants you to give away to others?

Imagine that within your spirit God has placed two baskets. As you begin your day, the Holy Spirit deposits in one basket what God wants you to give away that day. Each day the number and type of things deposited in your basket may vary, depending upon the needs that God wants you to touch and the people He wants you to bless.

Thank God today for what He placed within you and how He wants to use you.

Two Baskets (II)

Often, what the Holy Spirit deposits in your basket is a mystery. You do not know exactly what God has in mind for you during a day. The good news is that He doesn't ask you to try and figure it out or run around in circles trying to make everyone happy or meet everyone's needs. What He does want you to do is to be sensitive to the leading of the Holy Spirit and to respond to Him in simple faith and obedience.

As you go through your day, you may discover that the Holy Spirit has deposited within your basket a prayer He wants you to pray, a word of encouragement He wants you to speak, a blessing He wants you to give, or an act of kindness He wants you to extend.

Two Baskets (III)

Whatever it is that the Holy Spirit has deposited in your basket is what He desires for you to give away during your day. When you go to bed at night, it is good to have an empty basket. Nothing needs to be carried over, because the Holy Spirit will make new and fresh deposits each morning.

Earlier, I said there were two baskets that God has placed in your spirit. The second basket does not contain the things you give away during the day but the things that you receive from God that enrich your life and refresh your spirit. When you bless others, you are blessed; when you give out, you receive; when you empty yourself, you are filled. Consider the following Scriptures as ways God fills your other basket:

He who refreshes others will himself be refreshed.
– Proverbs 11:25 NIV –

"Give, and it will be given to you. A good measure, pressed down, shaken together and running over, will be poured into your lap. For with the measure you use, it will be measured to you."
– Luke 6:38 NIV –

Jesus – Ever Near, Forever Glorious

Jesus, ever near me, ever looking on; seeing my intentions before He beholds my failures; knowing my desires before He sees my faults; cheering me to endeavor greater things, and yet accepting the least; inviting my poor service, and yet, above all, content with my poorer love. The humblest and the simplest, the weakest and the most encumbered, may love Him not less than the busiest and strongest, the most gifted and laborious. If our heart be clear before Him; if He be to our chief and sovereign choice, dear above all, and beyond all desired; then all else matters little. That which concerns us He will perfect in stillness and in power.

– HENNY E. MANNING

What is highest in this world is lowest in the other, and what is highest in that world is lowest in this. Gold is on top here; they pave the streets with it there. To serve is looked upon as ignoble here; there those that serve reign and the last are first. I never saw a girl unwilling to fling away paste diamonds when she could have real stones, and when a man understands what God can be to the soul, he is independent of things he used to care for most.

– FREDERICK B. MEYER

Live in the Atmosphere of Peace

The work of righteousness will be peace,
and the effect of righteousness, quietness
and assurance forever. My people will
dwell in a peaceful habitation, in secure
dwellings, and in quiet resting places.
– Isaiah 32:17-18 –

Joy is a flame of the Holy Spirit within us. Fretting is like a giant fire extinguisher that seeks to quench the flame. The peace of God is the atmosphere that He wants us to live in. We need to guard against letting the news headlines, current events, the circumstances of life, or the worries and fears of others carry us outside of the atmosphere of God's peace.

God with Us

The LORD of hosts is with us.
– Psalm 46:7 –

God is with us, in good times and bad times; easy times and hard times; gentle times and turbulent times. When we face difficulties, God will sometimes remove them, sometimes He will show us the way to avoid them, and other times He will show us the way through them.

Having God's presence is more important than the circumstances we face or the people that are around us. When God tells you He will walk through something with you it means you have all you need – peace is there, strength is there, grace is there, love is there, because He is there.

Feed My Sheep (I)

Jesus said to him the third time, Simon, son of John, do you love Me [with a deep, instinctive, personal affection for Me, as for a close friend]? Peter was grieved (was saddened and hurt) that He should ask him the third time, Do you love Me? And he said to Him, Lord, You know everything; You know that I love You [that I have a deep, instinctive, personal affection for You, as for a close friend]. Jesus said to him, Feed My sheep.
– John 21:17 AMP –

After His resurrection, Jesus told Peter, "Feed my sheep." It was a clear and simple command that focused on Peter's responsibility to feed God's people. The term "sheep" is commonly used in Scripture to identify those who belong to the Lord. David speaks of it in the twenty-third Psalm, Isaiah speaks of it in chapter fifty-three, Jeremiah speaks of it in chapter fifty, and Jesus speaks of it in the tenth chapter of John. The term "feed" can include the idea of tending and caring for the sheep, but it also carries the responsibility of actually providing the food that sheep need to live on. Today, God wants you to be fed and He will provide what you need to feast upon.

Feed My Sheep (II)

What does food for God's people look and taste like? There are two main things that cannot be left out of any spiritual diet. One is the person (the life) of Jesus and the other is the words of Jesus. The Scriptures never separate what Jesus did from what Jesus said. In Acts 1:1 we read, "All that Jesus began both to do and teach."

Regarding His person, Jesus said, "I am the bread of life. I am the living bread which came down from heaven: if any man eat of this bread, he shall live for ever" (John 6:50-51). Regarding His words, Jesus said, "The words that I speak to you are spirit, and they are life" (John 6:63).

Jesus also said, "Man shall not live by bread alone, but by every word of God" (Luke 4:4). As new believers we need to feed on the milk of the Word (1 Peter 2:3). As we mature we need to feed on the meat of the Word (1 Corinthians 3:2).

The prophet Jeremiah said this about God's words, "Your words were found, and I ate them; and Your words were to me a joy and the rejoicing of my heart, for I am called by Your name, O Lord God of hosts" (Jer. 15:16).

Feed My Sheep (III)

We taste Thee, O Thou Living Bread,
And long to feast upon Thee still:
We drink of Thee, the Fountainhead
And thirst our souls from Thee to fill.

— ST. BERNARD OF CLAIRVAUX

God's sheep cannot be fed on people's opinions, on empty words, on meaningless rhetoric, on secular points of view, or on humanistic thinking. Our food is Truth, the living Truth and the spoken Truth of Jesus Christ. We need to feed upon the Truth, not have discussions about the Truth. No one ever survived by talking about food or writing books about food. We can only survive by partaking of food.

Feed My Sheep (IV)

He who has no money, come, buy and eat!
Yes, come, buy [priceless, spiritual] wine and milk
without money and without price [simply for the
self-surrender that accepts the blessing]. Why do
you spend your money for that which is not bread,
and your earnings for what does not satisfy?
Hearken diligently to Me, and eat what is good,
and let your soul delight itself in fatness
[the profuseness of spiritual joy].
– Isaiah 55:1-2 AMP –

How do we, as the sheep of His pasture, eat His spiritual food? First, we eat by coming to His table and asking. God has promised that if we ask for Bread He will not give us a stone.

Second, we eat by surrendering to the Word and yielding to its authority.

Third, we eat by receiving the Word by faith with gratitude and thanksgiving. As long as we have a hungry heart we will always find God's banqueting table filled with everything that is needed to sustain us and delight us. He has freely given us all things to enjoy.

Jesus, Our Beloved

And we have known and believed the love that God has for us.

— 1 JOHN 4:16

We are His beloved. Let us but feel that He has set His love upon us, that He is watching us from those heavens with tender interest, that He is working out the mystery of our lives with solicitude and fondness, that He is following us day by day as a mother follows her babe in his first attempt to walk alone, that He has set His love upon us, and, in spite of ourselves, is working out for us His highest will and blessing, as far as we will let Him, and then nothing can discourage us.

— A. B. SIMPSON

Jesus is King for us, Priest for us, and Prophet for us. Whenever we read a new title for our Redeemer, let us appropriate Him as ours in that name also. He is the Shepherd, the Captain, the Prince, and the Prophet. Jesus has no dignity which He will not employ for our exaltation and no prerogative which He will not exercise for our defense. His fullness in the Godhead is our unfailing, inexhaustible treasure house.

— CHARLES H. SPURGEON

No Fear

God won't say or do anything for the purpose of frustrating you, making you anxious, causing you to panic, or filling you with fear.

The Bible says, "The just shall live by faith," it doesn't say, "The just shall live by fear." The Word of God builds faith; fear builds worry.

Count on God in everything you do, in every circumstance you're in, in every need you face, in every decision you make. Never think about anything apart from Him.

With and Without (I)

Without Christ ... having no hope
and without God in the world.
– Ephesians 2:11 –

"I am with you always."
– Matthew 28:20 –

Being without certain things can be frustrating. A car without gas cannot take you where you want to go; a house without air conditioning cannot give you any relief from a heat wave.

Being without the more important things in life can be devastating. No one wants to live without the love and care of family, the availability of food, or the supply of clean drinking water.

By far, the worst imaginable thing is to be without God. To live without God is to live without discovering why you were made. To live without God is to be without hope, to be without light, and to be without reality. To be without God means that you can have it all and still be empty; you can protect yourself with every possible security and still not have peace; you can receive every type of reward and recognition and still be searching for meaning and purpose.

With and Without (II)

The best news we could ever hear is that we do not have to live without God. Jesus Christ came to earth to make atonement for our sins and to bring us back to God. Because He came, died, and rose again, we never have to live another day without Him. Jesus' words are amazing: "I am with you always!" Today your heart can soar, your voice can praise, and every fiber of your being can respond with celebration. You are not abandoned. You are not isolated. You are not an orphan. You are not an outcast. You are the Lord's!

With God, you may be broke, but you have the greatest riches; you may be single but you are not alone; you may walk through sorrow, but you have comfort; you may face difficulty, but you have hope; you may know your weakness, but you have strength; you may be unrecognizable to most people, but you are known by the Creator of the Universe.

Cast Your Cares on Him

"Cast your burden on the LORD, and He shall sustain you."

– PSALM 55:22

Worry, if carried to excess, has the nature of sin in it. The precept to avoid worry is repeated frequently by our Savior. It is reiterated by the apostles. It is a principle which cannot be neglected without involving transgression. We labor to take on ourselves our weary burden, as if He were unable or unwilling to take it for us. He who cannot calmly leave his affairs in God's hand is very likely to be tempted to use wrong means to help himself. Anxiety makes us doubt God's lovingkindness, and our love for Him grows cold. We feel mistrust and grieve the Spirit of God. If we cast each burden as it comes on Him and we are "careful for nothing" because He undertakes to care for us, it will keep us close to Him.

– CHARLES H. SPURGEON

Jesus Is

Jesus is the:

- doctor's cure
- pharmacist's prescription
- athlete's prize
- baker's bread
- tailor's pattern
- builder's foundation
- musician's melody
- composer's symphony
- artist's palette
- writer's story
- poet's rhyme

Jesus Is

Jesus is the:

- traveler's pathway
- explorer's true north
- sailor's safe haven
- mountain climber's summit
- perfumer's fragrance
- jeweler's precious stone
- gardener's rose
- astronomer's morning star
- banker's riches
- counselor's wisdom
- lawyer's truth
- heart's delight

The Pilgrim's Journey (I)

Peter, an apostle of Jesus Christ,
to the pilgrims of the Dispersion ...
– 1 Peter 1:1 –

What does it mean to be on a pilgrim's journey? When we think of a journey we think of someone who is on the move. Movement, however, does not always mean that we are making progress or actually getting somewhere. We can walk on a treadmill for thirty minutes and still be in the same place where we started. We can do laps on a track and just be going around in circles.

Peter begins his first epistle by addressing the followers of Christ as pilgrims. When we think of the word "pilgrim" we think of someone on a journey. Every follower of Christ is on a journey through this world. In the words of the songwriter, "This world is not my home/I'm just passing through."

As a follower of Christ, you are on a spiritual journey through a dark and sinful world. However, this does not mean that you are wandering around in a fog without purpose, hope, or direction. As Christ's pilgrim, it means that you are someone who knows where God has placed you, what He wants you to do, where He wants you to be heading, and assured of how to get there.

The Pilgrim's Journey (II)

Many years ago a popular song included the words "I still haven't found what I'm looking for." Christ's pilgrim is not someone who is trying to find meaning or purpose in life, but someone who has found what he is looking for. Christ's pilgrim is on a journey from earth to heaven, and on the journey the pilgrim never walks alone or wanders about without a purpose.

The Bible tells us to seek the Lord, but it also tells us that if we seek Him we will find Him. The pilgrim that the Bible addresses in first Peter is not someone who is walking about trying to find God, but someone who walks with God, who knows God, and is being guided by God in every step he takes. The pilgrim is not looking "for his place in this world" because he has already found his place in Christ.

The pilgrim's purpose is Christ; the pilgrim's destiny is Christ; the pilgrim's progress is Christ. For the pilgrim, life is not about the journey, but about Christ, the author of the journey.

The Pilgrim's Journey (III)

Christ's pilgrim is not someone who is "looking for the answers," but someone who has found Christ to be the answer; not someone who is following Christ on his own terms, but someone who is following Christ on God's terms; not someone who is trying to figure out the meaning to life, but someone who has found Christ to be his life.

A pilgrim is someone who walks in obedience to God's words and is surrendered to His authority. A pilgrim has fully embraced the lordship of Christ and is fully committed to the will of Christ. A pilgrim is a person of faith who trusts the One he is following, who walks in hope, who is kept by the power of God, who greatly rejoices, and who lives in the anticipation of an inheritance that is incorruptible, undefiled and that does not fade away, reserved for the pilgrim at the end of his journey.

A New Song (I)

When the LORD brought back the captivity
of Zion, we were like those who dream.
Then our mouth was filled with laughter,
and our tongue with singing. Then they
said among the nations, "The LORD has done
great things for them." The LORD has done
great things for us, and we are glad.
– Psalm 126:1-3 –

God isn't pleased by our being miserable.

– A. W. TOZER

We all go through times of sadness, sorrow, and tears. God draws close to us in tenderness during those times. But God does not want us to live a tear-filled life. Tears are for the night, but joy comes in the morning. The Bible tells us to "Rejoice evermore." God wants His song to be in our hearts and His praise to be on our lips. We are to bless the Lord at all times. It brings life to our spirits to walk in the joy of the Lord. It is the Lord who gives us a garment of praise for the spirit of heaviness; it is the Lord who is the lifter of our heads; it is the Lord who brings us fullness of joy.

A New Song (II)

The following story is Linda Miller's testimony of how God brought back His song into her life:

For many years I was known as one with a song on my heart and praise on my lips. One day that song disappeared. For approximately 5 years that once swelling voice was often silent with no desire to sing. Those years were a very difficult season with numerous deaths of dreams, increased responsibilities, and very difficult changes and situations.

I knew my heart needed to be released and to burst forth with jubilant song. I heard God saying, "Be silent no more, break forth into jubilant song, release your heart in praise to Me, the one who has redeemed you." I asked some friends to pray for my release and for my song to return. It did! The joy of Jesus, the love of Jesus and praise to God began returning to my heart more and more.

God has released the troubled heart that held the song captive. I testify with the psalmist in Psalm 40:2-4, "He also brought me up out of a horrible pit … He has put a new song in my mouth."

Obedience Is Always Best

In 1 Samuel 15 we discover that Saul was given a very clear command from the Lord. Saul did what the Lord commanded him, but not fully. Saul added something that God did not tell him to do. When Samuel confronted Saul with his disobedience, Saul tried to explain. Samuel was not impressed with Saul's explanation and told Saul, "Has the LORD as great a delight in burnt offerings and sacrifices as in obeying the voice of the LORD? Behold, to obey is better than sacrifice" (1 Sam. 15:22).

What is the best thing we can do as we follow the Lord? The answer is simple. The best thing we can do is what we have been asked to do. God does not want us to complicate things or put our own spin on it. Not doing what God asks us to do is disobedience, but adding something to what God has asked us to do is also disobedience. Let us walk with Him daily in simple trust and full obedience of faith.

"Whatever He Says to You, Do It"

"Whatever He says to you, do it."
– John 2:5 –

When the apostle Paul first met Jesus on the road to Damascus, he asked a very simple question, "What do you want me to do?" Paul spent the rest of his life doing what Jesus asked him to do.

What is Jesus asking you to do? How does He want you to spend this day? His guidance will always lead you into His provision.

As you do what He asks, you will find His grace to be sufficient, His strength to be abundant, His provision to be complete, His peace to be abiding, and His presence to be enough.

A Prayer of Surrender

Lord, take control of this day,
whatever You want is what I want to do –
I may not understand it
but I want You to tell me what You want of me.
This day I am turning over to You my thoughts, my plans,
my family, my work – everything. Amen.

His timing is always perfect, precise, and exact. He is always on time. He may change our schedules because our schedules don't match up to His – His thoughts and ways are higher than ours. When He makes changes, sometimes we feel like the rug's been pulled out from underneath us, but that's okay because we are to live in the Spirit. It's an exciting life ... when you are living in the Spirit, God can do anything He wants at any moment of the day.

– BEVERLY LESSIN

I Am Persuaded (I)

*For I am persuaded beyond doubt (am sure) that
neither death nor life, nor angels nor principalities,
nor things impending and threatening nor things
to come, nor powers, nor height nor depth, nor anything
else in all creation will be able to separate us from
the love of God which is in Christ Jesus our Lord.*
– Romans 8:38-39 AMP –

*And this is why I am suffering as I do. Still I am
not ashamed, for I know (perceive, have knowledge of,
and am acquainted with) Him Whom I have believed
(adhered to and trusted in and relied on), and I am
[positively] persuaded that He is able to guard and
keep that which has been entrusted to me and which
I have committed [to Him] until that day.*
– 2 Timothy 1:12 AMP –

Are you persuaded? What about? Not wishing about,
not wondering about, not hoping for the best about,
but persuaded about? They are the things that become
your foundations and what you build your life upon.
Can you identify the truths about which you are fully
persuaded?

I Am Persuaded (II)

Here are a few things you can be persuaded about:

- God's plans are the best plans and the right plans for your life.
- No one has a plan that is greater or wiser than God's plans for your life.
- God wants you to trust in Him with all your heart to fulfill those plans.
- God never makes a mistake because His plans are made with perfect wisdom.
- Every decision God makes for your life is a loving decision because God is love.
- Every decision God makes for your life is a good decision because God is good.
- God will never leave you nor forsake you. Therefore, you do not need to be afraid or worry about where God's plan will take you.

His Sound Is Like No Other

'Tis the sound of Jesus that rings softly in my ears.

'Tis the sound of Jesus that rings loudly in my heart.

'Tis the sound of Jesus that brings me to His feet.

'Tis the sound of Jesus that beckons me to His further paths.

'Tis the sound of Jesus that I know makes me sing.

Oh I sing the song of Jesus, ringing me , bringing me, beckoning me to higher praise.

'Tis the softness of His voice, my forever dance.

– LYDIA NAST

You Are the Lord's

*My substance was not hid from Thee, when I
was made in secret. Thine eyes did see my substance,
yet being unperfect; and in Thy book all my members
were written. How precious also are Thy thoughts
unto me, O God! how great is the sum of them!
If I should count them, they are more in number
than the sand: when I awake, I am still with Thee.*
– Psalm 139:15-18 *KJV* –

It is no accident that you are alive today. He has made no mistakes concerning you. He has given you all the light you need to know His will, and He has given you all the grace you need to do His will. He knows everything about you – your ups and downs, your highs and lows. He knows your thoughts, He knows your heart, and He is acquainted with all your ways. He has laid His hand of blessing upon you, and has placed His covering over you. He knows you by name and calls you His own.

No one knows you better or loves you more. Today, you are in God's place, in God's time, to fulfill God's plan, in God's way, by God's grace, for God's glory.

God Is Too Awesome Not to Be Trusted

God is above all things, beneath all things, outside of all things and inside of all things. God is above, but He's not pushed up. He's beneath, but He's not pressed down. He's outside, but He's not excluded. He's inside, but He's not confined. God is above all things presiding, beneath all things sustaining, outside of all things embracing and inside all things filling. That is the immanence of God.

– A. W. TOZER

"The people are to go out each day and gather enough for that day.

– EXODUS 1

"Enough for that day." That word completely takes away all care for tomorrow. Only today is yours; tomorrow is the Father's. Manna, as your food and strength, is given only by the day; to faithfully fill the present is your only security for the future. His presence and grace enjoyed today will remove all doubt as to whether you can entrust tomorrow to Him, too. Each new morning, He meets you with the promise of sufficient manna for the day.

– ANDREW MURRAY

The Right Thing

Embracing God's wisdom
 will help us know the right thing;
Embracing God's truth
 will help us believe the right thing;
Embracing God's holiness
 will help us choose the right thing;
Embracing God's righteousness
 will help us do the right thing;
Embracing God's majesty
 will help us focus on the right thing;
Embracing God's compassion
 will help us express the right thing;
Embracing God's character
 will help us become the right thing;
Embracing God's heart
 will help us love the right thing.

August

Secure and Certain (I)

*But know this, that in the last
days perilous times will come.*
– 2 Timothy 3:1 –

We are living in times of great uncertainty. The Bible makes it clear that there is only one thing that cannot be shaken; the kingdom of God. Everything about His kingdom is solid, unmovable, unshakeable, incorruptible, and undefiled.

The wise person is one who is building his life on the person of Jesus Christ, on the truth of His words, and on the reality of His kingdom.

In the uncertain times in which we are living, God wants us to live as people of faith and not people of "sight". We are to be people who live amidst fear, yet have peace; people who live amidst sorrow, yet have joy; people who live amidst trouble, yet have comfort; people who live amidst uncertainties, yet have hope.

Secure and Certain (II)

People of faith in God are not people who have found a way to avoid uncertainties or escape trouble. They are people who have learned to live in this world, but not be of it; to face difficulties and overcome them; to face hardships and walk through them. God is their security. Their trust is in God's character, their confidence is in God's ways, their hope is in God's promises, their joy is in God's presence, their strength is in God's power, and their stability is in God's kingdom.

In an uncertain world, God is the God of certainties. The certainties of God provide the anchor for every believer's soul. They pave the path for the pilgrim on his journey home; they are the covering for the soldier as he goes into battle; they are the blueprints that the carpenter uses to build his house; they are the track shoes that the sprinter uses as he runs for the finish line; they are the seeds that the gardener sows into the good soil of his heart as he awaits the final harvest.

Secure and Certain (III)

God has not made the earth and then abandoned it. He has not retreated somewhere in the universe and gone into hiding. He is today where He has always been, on His throne. God sees all things, knows all things, and is all-powerful. God is all in all. He is above all. Nothing is above Him or equal to Him. There is no king or ruler that has more authority than God; there is no political figure that has more influence than God; there is no nation that has more control than God. No one can out-think Him, or out-smart Him. He is God Almighty. He has all authority in heaven and earth. His enemies are under His feet. He reigns and rules. He is the majesty on High.

Thy throne, O God, is for ever and ever: the sceptre of Thy kingdom is a right sceptre.
– Psalm 45:6 KJV –

God reigneth over the heathen: God sitteth upon the throne of his Holiness.
– Psalm 47:8 KJV –

Secure and Certain (IV)

One God and Father of all, who is above all,
and through all, and in you all.
– Ephesians 4:6 KJV –

God has a plan and a purpose for everything that He has made. Everything is for His glory. All things were made by Him and for Him, and He is working all things out according to the council of His own will. He doesn't need a consulting firm to give Him any tips. He doesn't need any university professors to give Him any guidance. He doesn't need any religious leaders to give Him any counsel.

In the days in which we live God has a plan for His people, the body of Christ; He has a plan for the nations; He has a plan for your life. God is working out His plan. Nothing can stop His plan or frustrate His purposes. God is not worried about what will happen or what He will be able to do. God knows what will happen and He knows what He will do. Nothing takes Him by surprise. He sees the future and He is already there. He knows where He is leading your life and He knows how to get you there in His perfect time and way.

The Love List (I)

Let love be without hypocrisy. Abhor what is evil;
cling to what is good. Be devoted to one another in
brotherly love; give preference to one another in honor;
not lagging behind in diligence, fervent in spirit,
serving the Lord; rejoicing in hope, persevering in
tribulation, devoted to prayer, contributing to the
needs of the saints, practicing hospitality.
– Romans 12:9-13 NASB –

In our walk with God, there are things that He does and there are things that we do. In Romans 12:9-14 Paul gives us a list of things that we do. We don't do them apart from God, but we do them through Him, unto Him, and because of Him.

Paul makes it clear that the things we do are an outflow of the love that God has put within us. He tells us that our love should be genuine, a real and sincere manifestation of the love of God. God's love in us is expressed through us in various ways – through our words, our attitudes, our actions, our choices, and our character.

The Love List (II)

*Nevertheless the foundation of God standeth sure,
having this seal, The Lord knoweth them that
are his. And, Let every one that nameth
the name of Christ depart from iniquity.*
– 2 Timothy 2:19 KJV –

Abhor what is evil ...

It's okay to hate and detest certain things, to have nothing to do with them, and to keep them as far away from us as possible. Evil is one of those things (You who love the LORD, hate evil! [Ps. 97:10]). Anything that is devilish, bad, lewd, malicious, or wicked is evil.

If evil tries to get close to us we must push it away, if it tries to get in our thoughts we must reject it, if it tries to make us fearful we must not give it any ground. The answer to evil is always "no" and it is something we should always flee from.

The Love List (III)

*Now our Lord Jesus Christ Himself, and God,
even our Father, which hath loved us, and
hath given us everlasting consolation and good
hope through grace, comfort your hearts, and
stablish you in every good word and work.*
– 2 Thessalonians 2:16-17 KJV –

Cling to what is good ...

God not only wants us to run away from what is evil, but He also wants us to run toward what is good. Goodness is something we are to wrap our arms around and fully embrace. Our relationship with goodness should never be an indifferent one, a casual one, or an occasional one. We are to have a superglue relationship with the things that are good, creating a bond from which we cannot be pulled away.

The Love List (IV)

*My little children, let us not love in word
or in tongue, but in deed and in truth.*
– 1 John 3:18 –

Be devoted to one another in brotherly love ...

One of the things that believers have in common is that we are all members one of the same family. Being devoted to one another is an expression of the tender care that is common among those who live together in a family. Being devoted to one another in love means to give genuine affirmation, express deep appreciation, and convey heartfelt affection to those who are our brothers and sisters in Christ.

The Love List (V)

Render therefore to all their dues: tribute to
whom tribute is due; custom to whom custom;
fear to whom fear; honour to whom honour.
– Romans 13:7 KJV –

Give preference to one another in honor ...

A practical way that we can honor others is to put their needs, their advancement, and their overall success above our own. We give preference to others, when through our example, we take the lead in demonstrating what it means to be considerate, respectful, and thoughtful.

The Love List (VI)

For this very reason, adding your diligence
[to the divine promises], employ every effort
in exercising your faith to develop virtue (excellence,
resolution, Christian energy), and in [exercising]
virtue [develop] knowledge (intelligence).
– 2 Peter 1:5 AMP –

Not lagging behind in diligence ...

God does not want us to become sluggish, bogged down, listless, or running late regarding the things that He asks us to do. We are not to be people who are burdensome or hard to deal with. Always be on time and up to date regarding the things of the Spirit.

Walk in the Spirit, at His pace, and stay in step.

The Love List (VII)

But Jesus called them to Himself and said,
"You know that the rulers of the Gentiles lord it
over them, and those who are great exercise authority
over them. Yet it shall not be so among you; but whoever
desires to become great among you, let him be your
servant. And whoever desires to be first among you,
let him be your slave. Just as the Son of Man
did not come to be served, but to serve,
and to give His life a ransom for many."
– Matthew 20:25-28 –

Fervent in spirit, serving the Lord ...

When we serve the Lord we enter into a love relationship that binds us to His heart for others. Our expressions of love are always done through Him and unto Him. It is something we do from the heart, not indifferently, not coldly, but from a spirit that is bubbling over with compassion and tender care.

The Love List (VIII)

*But let all those who take refuge and put their
trust in You rejoice; let them ever sing and shout
for joy, because You make a covering over them
and defend them; let those also who love Your
name be joyful in You and be in high spirits.*
– Psalm 5:11 AMP –

Rejoicing in hope ...

A serving heart is a happy heart that is filled with
the assurance of knowing that it is pleasing Him. A
servant of the Lord can walk in fullness of joy because
his confidence, expectations, and hope are in the Lord
and not in man.

The Love List (IX)

Look well to yourself [to your own personality]
and to [your] teaching; persevere in these things
[hold to them], for by so doing you will save
both yourself and those who hear you.
– 1 Timothy 4:16 AMP –

Persevering in tribulation ...

God wants His people to stick it out, even when things are tough. Every servant of the Lord will face various kinds of hardships, difficulties, testing, and trials. Just because we walk and serve out of love, it does not mean that everyone will receive or welcome that love. We also have an enemy who will try and hinder or discourage us from giving love. When we face persecution, whatever the form, we are to persevere in our love, never losing heart or hope. We must never give up doing what His love is calling us to do.

The Love List (X)

*First of all, then, I admonish and urge that
petitions, prayers, intercessions, and thanksgivings
be offered on behalf of all men, for kings and all
who are in positions of authority or high responsibility,
that [outwardly] we may pass a quiet and
undisturbed life [and inwardly] a peaceable one in
all godliness and reverence and seriousness in every
way. For such [praying] is good and right, and [it is]
pleasing and acceptable to God our Savior.*
– 1 Timothy 2:1-3 AMP –

Devoted to prayer ...

We are to pray and keep on praying. Prayer is not an afterthought or a last resort. Jesus said, "Men always ought to pray and not lose heart." Don't lose heart when you're knocking, asking, and seeking after God in prayer; don't lose heart when the needs are great; don't lose heart when you have to wait; don't lose heart because God may seem slow, because He is never late.

The Love List (XI)

"Give, and [gifts] will be given to you; good measure,
pressed down, shaken together, and running over,
will they pour into [the pouch formed by] the
bosom [of your robe and used as a bag]. For with
the measure you deal out [with the measure
you use when you confer benefits on others],
it will be measured back to you."
– Luke 6:38 –

Contributing to the needs of the saints ...

Those who care will be those who share. Within the body of Christ there will always be needs to meet. Often, God involves many people to meet the need of one person. It is important for us to know what we are to contribute. We may not be able to do everything, but we can do our part.

The Love List (XII)

*Do not forget or neglect or refuse to extend
hospitality to strangers [in the brotherhood –
being friendly, cordial, and gracious, sharing
the comforts of your home and doing your
part generously], for through it some have
entertained angels without knowing it.*
– Hebrews 13:2 AMP –

Practicing hospitality ...

There's an old saying that's fitting for hospitality, "If
there is room in the heart there is room in the home."
We don't need a big home to extend hospitality to others,
but we do need a big heart. It is the love of Jesus, not our
expensive dishes or fancy furnishings that will touch
the lives of those who come into our homes.

*Contribute to the needs of God's people [sharing in the
necessities of the saints]; pursue the practice of hospitality.*
– Romans 12:13 AMP –

Looking Unto Jesus (I)

*Looking unto Jesus the author
and finisher of our faith.*
– Hebrews 12:2 –

The lost look to Jesus
    and see the loving Savior.
The wayward look to Jesus
    and see the only Way.
The confused look to Jesus
    and see the perfect Truth.
The empty look to Jesus
    and see the abundant Life.
The meek look to Jesus
    and see the suffering Servant.
The humble look to Jesus
    and see the risen Lord.
The blind look to Jesus
    and see the glorious Light.
The bound look to Jesus
    and see the conquering Warrior.
The oppressed look to Jesus
    and see the triumphant King.
The wounded look to Jesus
    and see the healing Physician.

Looking Unto Jesus (II)

Looking unto Jesus the author and finisher of our faith.
– Hebrews 12:2 –

The needy look to Jesus
    and see the caring Shepherd.
The hungry look to Jesus
    and see the living Bread.
The restless look to Jesus
    and see the Prince of Peace.
The mistreated look to Jesus
    and see the Righteous Judge.
The defenseless look to Jesus
    and see the great High Priest.
The barren look to Jesus
    and see the fruitful Vine.
The homeless look to Jesus
    and see their Dwelling Place.
The poor look to Jesus
    and see their Unsearchable Riches.
The lonely look to Jesus
    and see the ever-present Friend.
The insufficient look to Jesus
    and see their All in All.

Our Riches in Christ

We would have been satisfied if He had allowed us to eat the crumbs of His bounty beneath the table of His mercy; but He will do nothing by halves. He makes us sit with Him and share the feast. Had Jesus given us some small pension from His royal chambers, we would have had cause to love Him eternally. But no, He wants His bride to be as rich as Himself. He will not have a glory or a grace in which she will not share. He has not been content with less than making us joint-heirs with Himself, so that we might have equal possessions.

– CHARLES H. SPURGEON

All I have is thine; I have given it to you in Christ. All the Holy Spirit's power and wisdom, all the riches of Christ, all the love of the Father; there is nothing that I have that is not thine. I am God, and I love thee.

– ANDREW MURRAY

His Peace Is Your Peace

*Peace I leave with you; My [own] peace
I now give and bequeath to you. Not as the
world gives do I give to you. Do not let your hearts
be troubled, neither let them be afraid. [Stop allowing
yourselves to be agitated and disturbed; and
do not permit yourselves to be fearful and
intimidated and cowardly and unsettled.]*
– John 14:17 AMP –

Christ lives in you, and He is not anxious.

His Life Is Your Life

Nowhere in God's plan for your life does He tell you to learn how to make it on your own.

Hear my cry, O God; Attend to my prayer.
From the end of the earth I will cry to You,
When my heart is overwhelmed;
Lead me to the rock that is higher than I.
For You have been a shelter for me,
A strong tower from the enemy.
I will abide in Your tabernacle forever;
I will trust in the shelter of Your wings.

– Psalm 61:1-4 AMP –

His Song Is Your Song

What can these anxious cares avail thee,
    These never-ceasing moans and sighs?
What can it help if thou bewail thee
    O'er each dark moment as it flies?
Our cross and trials do but press
    The heavier for our bitterness.
Sing, pray, and keep His ways unswerving;
    So do thine own part faithfully,
And trust His word, though undeserving,
    Thou yet shalt find it true for thee;
God never yet forsook at need
    The soul that trusted Him indeed.

– GEORGE C. NEUMARK

Destiny and the Will of God (I)

What does it mean to fulfill our destiny? Some define destiny as our future place in heaven; others define destiny as discovering our present purpose on earth. It is common to think of fulfilling our destiny as "reaching our full potential" or "being all that we can be." It is common to hear people say, "We must dare to dream big and accomplish our goals." This sounds very noble, but it can be misleading and bring a lot of frustration and disappointment into people's lives as they pursue self-fulfillment.

The word "destiny" can carry some highly challenging, motivating, and inspiring thoughts within people's minds. It can also carry some allusions of grandeur. Many want to do big things or great things for God, but not too many want to do the little things or the unnoticed things.

It is easy to assume that if people fulfill their destiny they will become important, popular, or influential. God's destiny for you has nothing to do with what people assume.

Destiny and the Will of God (II)

Some teach that our destiny is found when we fulfill certain opportunities God gives to us to achieve greatness. Our destiny is not fulfilled through opportunities God gives to us, but through our relationship with His Son, Jesus Christ. No one's true destiny can be realized without Christ. In 1 Corinthians 8:6, Paul defines our destiny in two distinctive ways – "We exist *for* Him" and "We exist *through* Him."

The person who is in Christ is not someone who is looking for opportunities to fulfill his destiny, but someone who has fulfilled his destiny and found his divine purpose because he is in Christ (there can't be a higher destiny). Being in Christ means that you are where you need to be, you don't need to look anywhere else or do anything else to "arrive" at your destined place.

Destiny and the Will of God (III)

There is a difference between fulfilling our destiny and doing the will of God. While God's destiny for each of us is the same (to be in Christ), His will for each person can be very different. The will of God may lead some to be in a private place and others to be in a public place; lead some to be rulers and others to be servants in Caesar's household; lead some into the marketplace and others to be keepers at home; lead some to the mission field and others to a local ministry.

The will of God for each of us is for Him alone to decide. The will of God for one woman may mean traveling around the country speaking at women's conferences; the will of God for another woman may mean staying at home full-time. This does not mean that the woman who travels and speaks has fulfilled her destiny and that the woman who stays at home has missed her destiny. God sent Corrie ten Boom to speak from pulpits all around the world, and he kept Susanna Wesley at home to raise up boys who would impact the lives of millions.

Destiny and the Will of God (IV)

The apostle Paul's destiny in Christ was glorious, but the will of God for Paul's life did not look very glamorous. Nevertheless, Paul whole-heartedly embraced the will of God regardless of the difficulties or what others thought of him. Here, in his own words, Paul gives us a clear picture of what it cost him to follow the will of God:

> For I think that God has displayed us, the apostles, last, as men condemned to death; for we have been made a spectacle to the world, both to angels and to men. We are fools for Christ's sake ... we are weak ... we are dishonored ... being reviled, we bless; being persecuted, we endure; being defamed, we entreat. We have been made as the filth of the world, the offscouring of all things until now (1 Cor. 4:9-13).

Never forget that today, your destiny is not to find some great thing to do, but to know Him, glorify Him, and enjoy Him forever. When you have finished your earthly journey and fulfilled God's will for your life, whatever it may be, your glorious destiny in Christ will continue on forever.

Prayer

The LORD is nigh unto all them that call upon
Him, to all that call upon Him in truth.
– Psalm 145:18 KJV –

You may not be mighty, but you can pray and see situations change by the hand of Him who is almighty.

You may not be influential, but you can pray and ask Him who raises up one ruler and puts down another to have His way in the affairs of men.

You may not know how to comfort or encourage someone who is hurting, but you can pray and touch the heart of Him who is the Father of all comfort.

You may not know how to protect yourself from evil, but you can pray and allow God to be your shield and defender.

You may not have a lot of resources, but you can pray and receive what you need from the treasure house of Him whose resources are unlimited.

A Prayer of Committal and Covering

Lord, make me strong in Your hands. May my goals be shaped by Your will; may my resolve be based in Your truth; may my resources be used for Your glory and the good of others.

Cover me with grace, shield me with mercy, and motivate me with love. I know that there is nothing greater than Your presence with me and Your favor upon me.

May I move ahead with faith and reliance upon You in all things and at all times. May I live in such a way that pleases You and blesses others.

Amen.

He will regard the prayer of the destitute,
and not despise their prayer.
– Psalm 102:17 KJV –

I waited patiently for the LORD; and
He inclined unto me, and heard my cry.
– Psalm 40:1 KJV –

In God We Trust

It is good for me to draw near to God.
I have put my trust in the Lord God.
– Psalm 73:28 KJV –

We can trust in God because His:

- kingdom is unshakable.
- throne is incorruptible.
- glory is indescribable.
- Word is infallible.
- greatness is unsearchable.
- power is invincible.
- favor is invaluable.
- grace is inexpressible.
- love is undeniable.

It's All About Him

It's not about our careers;
   it's about His call upon our lives (Matt. 16:24).
It's not about us living for ourselves;
   it's about Him living in us (Gal. 2:20).
It's not about improving ourselves;
   it's about Him transforming us (2 Cor. 5:17).
It's not about our self-image;
   it's about His glory (1 Cor. 10:31).
It's not about our abilities;
   it's about His power (Acts 1:8).
It's not about our resources;
   it's about His sufficiency (2 Cor. 3:5).
It's not about living for the applause of others;
   it's about living for His approval (2 Tim. 2:15).

Peace with God

Therefore – having being justified by faith, we have peace with God through our Lord Jesus Christ.
– Romans 5:1 –

Peace with God means that you stand before Him in quietness and rest knowing that everything between you and Him is all right. You once were strangers, but now you are friends. You once were an alien, but now you are a citizen of His kingdom. You once were an outsider, but now you are a part of His eternal family.

There are no walls or barriers between you ... no fences dividing you ... no gulfs separating you. Your back is no longer turned toward Him, but you stand face to face in communion and fellowship. He is your Father and you are His child.

September

Access to Grace

Therefore being justified by faith,
we have peace with God through our Lord
Jesus Christ: By whom also we have access
by faith into this grace wherein we stand,
and rejoice in hope of the glory of God.
– Romans 5:1-2 KJV –

Admission means that we have gained access to a particular thing. Most of the things we would like to gain admission to take either a ticket, or a personal invitation.

For the most part we cannot gain access without money or influence. God wants us to have access to His grace.

Our way into that grace is not by money or influence, but by faith. Faith means that anyone and everyone can be admitted into that grace – a grace that causes us to stand, that enables us to rejoice, and that gives us our eternal hope.

God Is for You (I)

This I know, that God is for me.
– Psalm 56:9 –

When David wrote Psalm 56 it was at a time of great difficulty. He was pressed between two enemies. As though in a vise, he was being squeezed by Saul from one side and by the Philistines from the other. At this time, David had no great army to rescue him and he sat on no royal throne. In the midst of this great pressure, David kept his trust in the One who could save him and deliver him from all his fears. We discover the foundation of David's faith when he declares, "In God, whose word I praise, in God I have put my trust; I shall not be afraid. What can mere man do to me?" (v. 11).

How could David make such a bold and confident statement in the midst of such adversity? David could trust in God to save him because he *knew* that God was for him. As we face adversities from the enemy and difficulties in life, it is vital for each of us to know some key things about God's character and our relationship with Him. One of these vital keys is found in the word "knowing." What is it that you know to be sure and certain? What is it that you can build your life upon, your faith can rest upon, and your heart can lean upon?

God Is for You (II)

"Knowing" does not mean "I hope so", "I think so" or "I pray so." It means far more than knowing something in your head as you would know various facts or trivia. It means to be absolutely, positively, convinced about something with all your mind, all your heart, and all your soul. It means to be so certain of something that you are willing to cast all your care, all your worry, all your fears, and your very life upon it.

Thankfully, as God's children, we don't have to guess or make up something about God's true thoughts toward us. One way the enemy can defeat us is to deceive us. He tells us lies with the hope that we will believe them. He will tell you that God is against you. He will try to persuade you that God is not your friend, but your enemy. If you believe this lie you will doubt God's love and care for you. If you doubt God's love and care, you will not be able to put your complete trust in Him.

God Is for You (III)

David's psalm was familiar to Paul when he wrote, "And we know that all things work together for good to those who love God, to those who are the called according to His purpose ... If *God is for* us, who can be against us?" (Romans 8:28-31).

God wants you to know with all certainty that He is for you. When you get up in the morning, He is for you. When you get stuck in traffic, He is for you. When you are under a deadline at work, He is for you. When people misunderstand you or say unkind things about you, He is for you. When the enemy says you're finished and you'll never make it, He is for you. When there are problems and when there is pain, God is for you. When things are changing and times are uncertain, God is for you. When needs are pressing and answers are perplexing, God is for you.

God is for you. Count on it! Believe it! Act like it! Live like it! Trust like it! Rejoice like it! Know it ... because He really, truly, absolutely, positively is for you!

God Is for You (IV)

The following thoughts are based upon the Scriptures written in Romans 8. It states with clarity and certainty the truth that God is for you.

He did not spare His Son, but delivered Him up for you – God is for you.

Through His Son He will freely give you all things – God is for you.

He will not bring a charge against you – God is for you.

You are His elect – God is for you.

Jesus makes intercession for you – God is for you.

You are more than a conqueror though Him who loves you – God is for you.

Nothing can separate you from His love – God is for you.

God Is for You (V)

God is for you.
  God is for you.
God is for you.
  God is for you.

What then shall we say to these things? If God is for us, who can be against us? He who did not spare His own Son, but delivered Him up for us all, how shall He not with Him also freely give us all things? (Rom. 8:31-32).

God Is for You (VI)

God gives you strength and power.
  God is for you (Ps. 68:35).

God is your deliverer.
  God is for you (Ps. 68:20).

God daily bears your burden.
  God is for you (Ps. 68:19).

God leads out the prisoners into prosperity.
  God is for you (Ps. 68:6).

God makes a home for the lonely.
  God is for you (Ps. 68:6).

God will not turn away your prayer.
  God is for you (Ps. 66:20).

God Is for You (VII)

God will not turn away His lovingkindness toward you.
God is for you (Ps. 66:20).

God shelters you under His wings.
God is for you (Ps.61:4).

God redeems your soul from the battle against you.
God is for you (Ps. 55:18).

God will deliver you from all trouble.
God is for you (Ps. 54:7).

God will guide your life.
God is for you (Ps. 48:14).

God gives you favor.
God is for you (Ps. 44:3).

God Is for You (VIII)

God's song will be with you in the night.
God is for you (Ps. 42:8).

God holds your hand.
God is for you (Ps. 37:24).

God's eyes are upon you.
God is for you (Ps. 34:15).

God's ears are open to your cry.
God is for you (Ps. 34:15).

God will bless you with peace.
God is for you (Ps. 29:11).

God will not forsake you, even when you are old and gray.
God is for you (Ps. 71:18).

God Is for You (IX)

God is for you no matter who is against you. If the devil tells you that God is against you, reject the lie and declare the truth, "God is for me, His Word declares it, the death of His Son upon the cross demonstrates it, and His mercy and grace affirm it every day to my heart."

God is for you, not because you have a nice personality, a great smile, a strong arm, a witty way, a clever disposition, self-discipline, or a lively imagination.

God is for you, not because you go to church, because you have added ten minutes to your prayer time, because you have increased your giving by five percent, or because you are memorizing Scripture.

God is for you, not because you try to be good, because you try hard, or because you try to always do your best;

God is for you because He has set His love upon you.

God Is for You (X)

God is for you when you walk through valleys. God is for you when you pass through troubled seas; God is for you when you are weak, when you are wounded, and when you are weary. God is for you when He disciplines and corrects you. God is for you when He molds and shapes you, when He prunes you, and when He purifies you.

God is for you in times of persecution, in times of difficulty, and in times of need. God is for you in low times and high times, in crooked paths and straight paths, in darkness and in the light of dawn's new day. God is for you when others set you aside, when you have been ignored, when you have been unappreciated, rejected, and when you have been mistreated.

God Is for You (XI)

God was for you when He formed you in the womb and gave you the breath of life. He was for you when you were born into this world. He was for you when He pursued you in your sin and rebellion. He was for you when He drew you to His side, to His arms, to His love, and to His heart. God was for you when He covered you with mercy, clothed you with grace, and called you His own.

God (the awesome, glorious, all-powerful, all-wise, majestic, magnificent, holy, eternal, righteous, caring, loving, King of the universe and Lord of all)

Is (not has been, not will be, not might be, not one day will be)

For (not against, not hostile toward, not contrary to, not indifferent to)

You (not just someone else, but you; not just other believers, but you; not part of you, but all of you!)

Declare it: God is for ME!

The King and His Kingdom in You

*For the Kingdom of God is not just
fancy talk; it is living by God's power.*
– 1 Corinthians 4:20 NLT –

The kingdom of God makes all the difference in you and in your day because you are a part of it. There is no kingdom, rule, or authority that is greater than God's kingdom. The kingdom of God is all about the reign of Jesus Christ in your life. Jesus is the King of the kingdom, and every benefit of the Kingdom is yours because you have the King ruling your life.

Jesus reigns and rules over everything that He has overcome, over everything He has defeated, and over everything He has conquered. Jesus is the triumphant King, the mighty Warrior, and the risen Lord. He faced the onslaughts of Satan's attacks and crushed them; He faced the temptations of sin and overcame them; He faced the grip of death and triumphed over it. Today, Jesus is your authority over the kingdom of darkness, He is your deliverer over the power of sin, and He is your victory over the fear of death.

His Kingdom Is Yours

Jesus' kingdom within you is unshakeable, indestructible, and impenetrable. Nothing can come against it and prevail; nothing can challenge it and win; nothing can defy it and overcome. The kingdom of God means that you do not have to live this day in your own strength, but by Jesus' power; not in your own efforts, but in Jesus' finished work; not in your own abilities, but in Jesus' endless resources.

If you are facing temptation today, resist it and let Jesus' victory be yours.

If the enemy is trying to pull you down and discourage you, let Jesus' strength lift you up and cause you to stand firm.

If you are facing fear or worry, let Jesus be your confidence, your hope, and your security.

If your life is broken, let Jesus make you whole.

Never Own Anything (I)

Dr. Tozer told the story of a farmer who planted his seed and prayed, "God, please bless my crops." However, at the time of harvest the farmer's crops failed. The following year the farmer planted his seed and once again prayed, "God, please bless my crops." Once again the crops failed.

The next year the farmer did as he had done the previous two years and prayed the same prayer, "God, please bless my crops." This time, however, the farmer did something different. After praying, he quieted his heart enough to hear God speak these words to him, "Whose crops?"

"God, please bless my crops," the farmer repeated.

"Whose crops?" God asked the farmer once again.

The farmer paused for a moment and then cried out, "I get it, Lord, I get it! God, bless *Your* crops."

That fall the farmer brought in an abundant harvest.

Never Own Anything (II)

The Bible tells us in 1 Corinthians 4:7, "What do you have that you did not receive?" Everything we have comes from God. We own nothing and should not try to take possession of anything or anyone. It is important for us to hold with an open hand, everything that God has placed into our lives, without seeking to possess it with a closed fist. God will freely give us all things to enjoy, but we cannot enjoy what He gives us if we do not release the ownership of it to Him.

Here are some wise words from Watchman Nee about ownership:

Can we trust God to keep for us what He has given, never laying hold on it ourselves in our natural desire for possession? What God gives, he gives! We need not struggle to retain it. Indeed if we grasp it fearfully and hold on, we may risk losing it. Only what we have let go of in committal to Him becomes in fact really ours.

Dependency

Clothe (apron) yourselves, all of you,
with humility [as the garb of a servant,
so that its covering cannot possibly be
stripped from you, with freedom from pride
and arrogance] toward one another.
– *1 Peter 5:5 AMP* –

To walk in humility before God we must understand our dependency upon God. There are many places in Scripture that illustrate our relationship of dependency upon Him. We are told that He is the True Vine and we are the branches; He is the Potter and we are the clay; He is the Shepherd and we are the sheep; He is the Head and we are the body; He is Giver and we are the receivers; He is the Master and we are His servants.

Without the Vine the branch would shrivel; without the Potter the clay would be without form; without a Shepherd the sheep would be without care; without the Head the body would die; without the Giver we would be empty; without a Master we would be left to our own way.

There Is One Who Cares for You

Let this quote from Charles H. Spurgeon encourage you today:

Oh, child of suffering, be patient. God has not passed you over in His providence. He who is the feeder of sparrows will also furnish you with what you need. Take up the arms of faith against a sea of trouble. There is One who cares for you. His eye is fixed on you, His heart beats with pity for your woe, and His omnipotent hand will bring you the needed help.

The darkest cloud will scatter itself in showers of mercy. The blackest gloom will give place to the morning. He, if you are one of His family, will bind up your wounds and heal your broken heart. Do not doubt His grace because of your tribulation, but believe that He loves you as much in seasons of trouble as in times of happiness.

With a little oil in the cruse and a handful of meal in the barrel, Elijah outlived the famine, and you will do the same.

John 16:33 (I)

"I have told you these things, so that in Me
you may have [perfect] peace and confidence. In the
world you have tribulation and trials and distress
and frustration; but be of good cheer [take courage;
be confident, certain, undaunted]! For I have
overcome the world. [I have deprived it of power
to harm you and have conquered it for you.]"

– AMP –

The following quote from E. Stanley Jones helps us to
focus on the depth of meaning in John 16:33.

"In the world you will have trouble. But courage!
The victory is mine; I have conquered the world"
(John 16:33 NEB). I have conquered the world – not
will conquer, but I have conquered. So every foe
of the Kingdom is a defeated foe before we get to
it. When sin and temptation come to bully me I ask
them to bend their necks and when they do, I say,
"Yes, I thought so. The footprint of the Son of God
is on your necks." So I by identification with Him
become victorious in His victory, strong in His
strength, pure in His purity, loving in His love. I
work from the victory to the victory.

John 16:33 (II)

Regardless of the times in which we live, there are certain things that we will face. The first thing is tribulation. This is nothing new. The church of Jesus Christ has been living through tribulation since its birth two-thousand years ago.

The second thing is that Jesus does not want us to place our focus on tribulation, but on Him. Jesus has overcome the world, but if we put our focus on tribulation, the world can easily overcome us with worry, fear and anxiety.

The third and fourth things are huge anchor points for us. Jesus tells us that even though we will have tribulation we can have His perfect peace; He also tells us that we are to be of good cheer. These two things, perfect peace and good cheer, should dominate our thinking, our speech, and our attitudes each day.

John 16:33 (III)

Nothing in this world has the power to take from you what Jesus wants to give you. It is Jesus who has conquered darkness and overcome the world. It is Jesus who is on the throne. It is Jesus who is working out His plan for your life.

Take Jesus' peace,
    He is not worried;
take His joy,
    He is not discouraged;
take His rest,
    He is not uptight;
take His victory,
    He is not defeated;
take His life,
    He is not dead.

He alone has all the power, all the peace, and all the good cheer you will ever need.

God Is Faithful

God does not want you to place your focus on your needs, but on His faithfulness; not on world problems, but on His faithfulness; not on circumstances, but on His faithfulness; not on your feelings or opinions, but on His faithfulness; not on political change, but on His faithfulness.

The truth of God's faithfulness is something each of us will need to be reminded of many times throughout our lives. Our faith needs to rest in His faithfulness; our feet need to stand upon His faithfulness; our heart needs to trust in His faithfulness; our emotions need to celebrate His faithfulness; our mouths need to proclaim His faithfulness.

"God is faithful."

God Is Faithful to You

God is faithful it's true
    He will make all things new,
Just trust Him to do
    All He's promised to you.
God is faithful.

Know, recognize, and understand therefore that the Lord your God, He is God, the faithful God, Who keeps covenant and steadfast love and mercy with those who love Him and keep His commandments, to a thousand generations (Deut. 7:9 AMP).

God is faithful (reliable, trustworthy, and therefore ever true to His promise, and He can be depended on); by Him you were called into companionship and participation with His Son, Jesus Christ our Lord (1 Cor. 1:9 AMP).

God is trustworthy and faithful and means what He says (2 Cor. 1:18 AMP).

O LORD God of Heaven's Armies! Where is there anyone as mighty as You, O LORD? You are entirely faithful (Ps. 89:8 NLT).

Mercy, Peace and Love

May you receive more and more of
God's mercy, peace, and love.
– Jude 1:2 (NLT) –

It's a new day ... you have never gone this way before.
What you have planned for today is not what makes it
meaningful. What makes it meaningful is that God is
in it.

He was in it when you first opened your eyes. He has
sustained you through the years, greeted you with new
mercies at morning's light, given you the breath of life,
and promised to direct your steps until your journey is
complete.

Because of God's mercies you can follow Him with
all of your heart this day, assured that there is nothing
being held over your head to condemn you; you can
take each step with a quiet heart knowing that His
peace keeps you steady and sure; you can move ahead
with great confidence of faith knowing His love keeps
you close to His heart, mindful of His promises, and
confident of His care.

God's Provisions for Today

Are you tired or weary?
    Allow God to renew you with His strength.
Are you discouraged or downhearted?
    Allow God to lift you with His love.
Are you carrying a burden of sin?
    Allow God's mercies to restore you.
Are you in need of reassurance?
    Allow God to hold you in His embrace.
Are you in need of healing?
    Allow God to mend you with His touch.

Today, you are His child and He is your Father – you belong to Him and He belongs to you; He matters to you and you matter to Him; you are committed to Him and He is committed to you. Today there is mercy, there is peace, and there is love.

The Good Shepherd

You, Lord, are my shepherd. I will never be in need.
You let me rest in fields of green grass.
You lead me to streams of peaceful
water, and You refresh my life.
You are true to Your name,
and You lead me along the right paths.
I may walk through valleys as
dark as death, but I won't be afraid.
You are with me, and Your shepherd's
rod makes me feel safe.
You treat me to a feast, while my enemies watch.
You honor me as Your guest, and
You fill my cup until it overflows.
Your kindness and love will always
be with me each day of my life, and I will
live forever in Your house, Lord.

– Psalm 23 CEV –

Humility

"I love being nothing so He can be my all."

– DON LESSIN

Those who walk before God in humility are:

- Weak enough to lean upon His strength;
- Small enough to look upon His greatness;
- Patient enough to wait upon His timing;
- Empty enough to draw upon His fullness;
- Poor enough to depend upon His riches;
- Needy enough to count upon His grace.

Freedom From Your Past

Do not [earnestly] remember the former things;
neither consider the things of old. Behold, I am doing
a new thing! Now it springs forth; do you not perceive
and know it and will you not give heed to it? I will even
make a way in the wilderness and rivers in the desert.
– Isaiah 43:18-19 AMP –

In order to move forward in God's plan and will for your life you must be free from your past. To move ahead with confidence is to know that there is a God who goes before you as your captain and your guide. To move ahead with freedom is to know that this same God is behind you as your rear guard to keep you from being defeated by any failures or disappointments of the past.

Follow Me

Then He said to them, "Follow Me,
and I will make you fishers of men."
– Matthew 4:19 –

When Jesus walks into your life,
He comes with scarred feet.

He comes as a servant,
He greets you with
a basin and a towel.

He calls you to follow Him
by taking your hand in His –
Letting His wounds assure you
that you will never walk the path
He has chosen for you without His presence.

Confidence

Confidence is not based on you having all the resources needed to take care of yourself; confidence is based upon the truth that God is faithful.

There is one thing that God says to every believer, regardless of his circumstances – "Trust Me."

Trust in the LORD, and do good; dwell in
the land, and feed on His faithfulness.
– Psalm 37:3 –

And they who know Your name [who have experience
and acquaintance with Your mercy] will lean on and
confidently put their trust in You, for You, Lord, have not
forsaken those who seek (inquire of and for) You [on the
authority of God's Word and the right of their necessity].
– Psalm 9:10 AMP –

October

There Is a Love

May Christ through your faith [actually]
dwell (settle down, abide, make His permanent home)
in your hearts! May you be rooted deep in love and
founded securely on love, that you may have
the power and be strong to apprehend and grasp with
all the saints [God's devoted people, the experience of that
love] what is the breadth and length and height
and depth [of it]; [That you may really come] to know
[practically, through experience for yourselves] the
love of Christ, which far surpasses mere knowledge
[without experience]; that you may be filled
[through all your being] unto all the fullness
of God [may have the richest measure of
the divine Presence, and become a body
wholly filled and flooded with God Himself]!
– Ephesians 3:17-19 AMP –

There is a love that reaches to the breadth of all you could ever desire, that accompanies you throughout the length of your life's journey, that reaches to the depths of your innermost being, and that takes you to the heights of all your heart can hold.

Desires

*You open your hand and satisfy
the desire of every living thing.*
– Psalm 145:16 –

It is much that He should satisfy the need, the want; but He goes far beyond that. Pity is moved to meet our need; duty may sometimes look after our wants; but to satisfy the desire implies a tender watchfulness, a sweet and gracious knowledge of us, an eagerness of blessing. God is never satisfied until He has satisfied our desires.

– MARK GUY PEARSE

Our desires to do the works of God can only be fulfilled by the hand of God; our desires for the knowledge of God can only be fulfilled by the revelation of God; our desires for the fellowship of God can only be fulfilled by the presence of God; our desires for the blessings of God can only be fulfilled by the favor of God; our desires for the power of God can only be fulfilled by the fullness of God.

The Flesh and the Spirit (I)

But I say, walk in the Spirit, and you
will not carry out the desire of the flesh.
For the flesh sets its desire against the Spirit,
and the Spirit against the flesh.
– Galatians 5:16-17 NASB –

My flesh said, "I want to pursue my goals."

The Spirit said, "Pursue my purposes."

My flesh said, "I have great ideas."

The Spirit said, "I have a perfect plan."

My flesh said, "I want to draw people by my personality."

The Spirit said, "I want to draw people by My presence."

My flesh said, "Look at my determination."

The Spirit said, "Let Me be in control."

My flesh said, "I have talent."

The Spirit said, "Desire My gifts."

My flesh said, "I am working hard."

The Spirit said, "Receive My power."

The Flesh and the Spirit (II)

My flesh said, "I have a great mind."
   The Spirit said, "Seek My wisdom."
My flesh said, "I want to make a difference."
   The Spirit said, "I am the difference."
My flesh said, "I am well educated."
   The Spirit said, "I will give you revelation."
My flesh said, "I am clever."
   The Spirit said, "I am truth."
My flesh said, "I want to be a person of influence."
   The Spirit said, "Walk in My favor."
My flesh said, "I want to keep trying new things."
   The Spirit said, "Drink of Me."
My flesh said, "I am a nice person."
   The Spirit said, "I am love."

The Flesh and the Spirit (III)

*And those who belong to Christ Jesus
(the Messiah) have crucified the flesh (the godless
human nature) with its passions and appetites
and desires. If we live by the [Holy] Spirit, let us
also walk by the Spirit. [If by the Holy Spirit we
have our life in God, let us go forward walking
in line, our conduct controlled by the Spirit.]*
– Galatians 5:24-25 AMP –

My flesh said, "I am doing the best I can."

The Spirit said, "Let Me do it through you."

My flesh said, "I am weary."

The Spirit said, "I will renew your strength."

My flesh said, "I am trying to live a good life."

The Spirit said, "I will make you holy."

My flesh said, "I need to be dynamic."

The Spirit said, "You need to be anointed."

My flesh said, "I want recognition."

The Spirit said, "Seek My approval."

My flesh said, "I want people to like me."

The Spirit said, "I want people to glorify Jesus."

My flesh said, "It's all about me."

The Spirit said, "It's all about Jesus."

Storm (I)

You rule the swelling of the sea;
when its waves rise, You still them.
– Psalm 89:9 –

The size and strength of a tsunami displays tremendous power. To see it move upon the land is staggering. The lesson is clear, when a tsunami is heading your way, you shouldn't be running to the beach to get a better view, or try clinging to a palm tree to wait out the storm. Run instead to the high ground, for it is there that you will find your refuge.

In Psalm 61:2 King David said, "Lead me to the rock that is higher than I." David knew where to flee in times of danger. Like David, we must not think that we are smarter or stronger than the storms in life that come against us. We cannot outrun them or outsmart them. Our enemies are too strong for us to come against them with naive zeal or human determination. Our victory over every storm of life must be found in the Lord.

Storm (II)

The psalmist tells us in Psalm 9:9-10, "The LORD also will be a refuge and a high tower for the oppressed, a refuge and a stronghold in times of trouble." God is the One we run to when the storm comes, and He is also our high tower on the high ground. In Him we are doubly sheltered. God is not only the most strategic place to be in any storm, but He is also the most secure place to be.

We should not only run to God and hide in Him when we face any storm, but we should also trust in Him to rule the storm and command it to be still. God never tells us to wait or delay our running to Him and taking shelter in Him, however, this does not mean that God will immediately command the storm to be still. God does not tell us to delay running to Him, but He may have a reason to delay taking action against the storm. There are reasons for God's delays that we may never know or fully understand, but He asks us to trust Him while we wait. Because we are safe in Him, we can wait without apprehension until the winds have been calmed, until the waves have stopped swelling, and until the storm has been made still.

Storm (III)

And therefore will the LORD wait, that He
may be gracious unto you, and therefore
will He be exalted, that He may have mercy
upon you: for the LORD is a God of judgment:
blessed are all they that wait for Him.
– Isaiah 30:18 –

"This is God's way. In the darkest hours of the night His tread draws near across the billows. As the day of execution is breaking, the angel comes to Peter's cell. When the scaffold for Mordecai is complete, the royal sleeplessness leads to a reaction in favor of the threatened race.

Ah, soul, it may have come to the worst with thee ere thou art delivered; but thou wilt be! God may keep thee waiting, but He will ever be mindful of His covenant, and will appear to fulfill His inviolable Word."

– FREDERICK B. MEYER

Stability

He will be the stability of your times.
– Isaiah 33:6 –

Uncertainty is all about us. Things that seemed secure have become unstable, foundations that seemed like rocks have turned into sand, and confidence has turned into confusion. Many people have looked for security and stability in places that seemed safe and secure, but these places have proven to be unable to bear up under the pressures of our times.

Only God can be our stability in an unstable world and our certainty in uncertain times. Only God knows what is ahead for us and where we are going. Only God can speak to us with the voice of certainty and say, "This is the way, walk ye in it" (Isa. 30:21).

"Work Out"

*Therefore, my dear ones, as you have always
obeyed [my suggestions], so now, not only [with the
enthusiasm you would show] in my presence but much
more because I am absent, work out (cultivate, carry
out to the goal, and fully complete) your own salvation
with reverence and awe and trembling (self-distrust, with
serious caution, tenderness of conscience, watchfulness
against temptation, timidly shrinking from whatever
might offend God and discredit the name of Christ).*
– Philippians 2:12 AMP –

Step out in faithful obedience;
    Speak out the words of life and hope;
Move out in His grace and mercy;
    Reach out in prayer;
Live out what He is working within you;
    Give out all He has freely given you;
Cast out every fear and bondage of the enemy;
    Keep out all that is displeasing in His sight;
Pour out a sacrifice of thanksgiving and praise.

Sanctified Imaginations

We need sanctified imaginations. It is easy for any of us to fret and have our imaginations run wild. In reality, most things don't happen the way we imagined them.

The Bible says, "The just shall live by faith" (Rom. 1:17). It doesn't say, "The just shall live by their imaginations." The Word of God builds your faith; your imagination can be a fast track to worry. Worry says, "What will happen to me, things seem out of control." Faith says, "My life is in God's hands and He is in control."

Wisdom

O Lord, how manifold are Thy works! In wisdom hast
Thou made them all: the earth is full of Thy riches.
– Psalm 104:24 kjv –

God is wise. Everything He does for you is done in wisdom. Every decision He makes on your behalf is done in wisdom.

God has perfect wisdom, which means that it is impossible for Him to make a mistake. God's wisdom is complete. He never gains wisdom or grows in wisdom, because He has all wisdom.

God's wisdom means that He works in very practical ways in your life.

God is your wise mentor, your practical helper, and your patient instructor.

God's hands are more skilled than a great surgeon;
    They are more assuring than a caring nurse;
    They are more precise than a fine diamond cutter;
    They are more creative than the finest artist or designer.

Be Still

"Be still, and know that I am God."
– Psalm 46:10 –

The government (the rule and reign of your life) is upon His shoulders. He hasn't placed any of it on yours. He has a plan and purpose for your life and He not only knows where He is taking you, but He also knows how to get you there.

God is in control. Things won't always be the way they are right now.

God knows how and when to bring about change. Trust His timing, He doesn't err.

"Have Joy" (I)

"Have a good time" and "have fun" are common sayings we use with one another. It's not a bad thing to say to someone, but it does have its limitations. How about if we replace "have fun" with "have joy." Joy is one of the greatest things we can possess on earth and differs greatly from fun.

"Fun" is fine, but we can't always have fun. Fun depends so much on where we are in a given moment and what we are doing. It's not fun to be caught in a traffic jam, to have a financial set back, to go through a difficult trial, to be without heat in the winter, or to have a mechanical breakdown when you are trying to meet a deadline. It's fun to go skiing, but it's not fun to break your leg. It's fun to watch a baseball game, but it's not fun to watch your team lose. It's fun to eat at a nice restaurant, but it's not fun to get food poisoning. It's fun to hook a big trout, but it's not fun to have it get away.

Why do so many look for fun when they could have joy?

"Have Joy" (II)

Joy is a grace gift from God, not the result of a particular circumstance that happens in our lives. Joy touches our spirits, fun touches our emotions; joy abides, fun comes and goes; joy flows like deeps waters, fun skips along like a rock upon the water's surface.

Joy is amazing and strength giving. Joy isn't just for the good times, but for the hard times as well. Jesus knew joy even while going through the agony and suffering of the cross. The joy that Jesus knew is the joy we need to know as we face every circumstance of life – hard or easy, bad or good, difficult or pleasant – and it is His joy that He gives to us.

"Have Joy" (III)

Now may the God of hope fill you with all joy.
– Romans 15:13 –

A Christian homemaker with the gift and ministry of hospitality was taught an important lesson by the Lord when she was a young missionary. She was once served a meal of tortillas and eggs by a Christian woman who lived in an adobe house with dirt floors, in the back country of Mexico. Her hostess had so little to offer materially and yet she radiated joy in everything she did. To this day, the Christian homemaker was never served more graciously. She learned that the joy of hospitality is not in having a modern kitchen or beautiful dishes, but in bringing the graciousness of Christ to those who gather at your table.

Whatever your day might bring, "Have joy"; whatever your circumstances, "Have joy"; whatever you need, "Have joy." Have God's joy. Have it in abundance. Have it in its fullness. Be filled with joy. Have the joy of His presence, and the joy of His salvation. May His joy greet you at the start of each step of obedience, meet you at the end of every tear, cover you in every trial, and sustain you in every labor of love. May His joy remain.

"Have joy!"

Bread (I)

"Our forefathers ate the manna in the wilderness; as the Scripture says, He gave them bread out of heaven to eat. Jesus then said to them, I assure you, most solemnly I tell you, Moses did not give you the Bread from heaven [what Moses gave you was not the Bread from heaven], but it is My Father Who gives you the true heavenly Bread. For the Bread of God is He Who comes down out of heaven and gives life to the world. Then they said to Him, Lord, give us this bread always (all the time)! Jesus replied, I am the Bread of Life. He who comes to Me will never be hungry."
– John 6:31-35 AMP –

Jesus is Bread. He doesn't have bread to give us; He is the Bread He gives us.

He is the Bread of the Passover – Unleavened. Striped. Pierced.

He is the Bread of the Tabernacle – Made with fine flour. Bread of the assembly and Bread of the individual. The Bread of God's presence, whose face shines upon you.

He is the Bread of Bethlehem – Sent from Heaven. Given for all who receive.

He is the broken Bread – the Bread of Emmaus, the Bread of Melchizedek, the Bread of the wilderness.

Bread (II)

Bread is not made to be displayed, to be admired, to be studied, to be analyzed, to be compared with other breads, to be used as a center piece, or to be packaged. Bread is not made to educate or entertain; it is made to sustain. Bread is to be eaten.

Jesus is the Living Bread. He is the Bread of communion, the Bread of fellowship, the Bread of covenant, the Bread of healing and wholeness, the Bread of intimacy, the Bread of revelation, and the Bread of blessing.

By faith, receive Him, eat of Him, delight in Him, partake of Him. He is fresh Bread, daily Bread.

Take as much as you can, again and again, there will always be enough and more than enough.

Bread (III)

Jesus is Bread baked in the oven of affliction. The Bread of our sorrows and the Bread of our tears. He is the Bread of all mercies, the Bread of all compassion, and the Bread of all grace.

- Bread of life.
- Bread of glory.
- Bread of beauty.
- Bread of health.
- Bread of deliverance.
- Bread of joyful journeys.

Bread of Heaven, feed me ... nourish my soul ... fill my hunger ... be my strength. Be in every fiber of my being, in every heartbeat, in every longing, in every hope, in every work, in every step, in every plan, in every purpose.

Amen

Our Home (I)

*That is what the Scriptures mean when they say,
"No eye has seen, no ear has heard, and no mind has
imagined what God has prepared for those who
love Him." But it was to us that God revealed these
things by His Spirit. For His Spirit searches
out everything and shows us God's deep secrets.*
– 1 Corinthians 2:9-10 NLT –

Jesus came to us from heaven, lived among us, and returned to heaven. Heaven is His home and it is ours. Jesus talked a lot about heaven and told us that He was going there to prepare a place for us, and what a place it must be!

One of the things that the Holy Spirit is working within the hearts of God's people is the knowledge that heaven is greater than anything we have ever thought about or imagined. Reading books about heaven, looking at paintings about heaven, or even listening to stories about heaven don't help us very much. These sources are much too limited to give us a full account.

Our Home (II)

The Bible mentions heaven many times, but it does not tell us a lot about the details of heaven. The Scripture passage in 1 Corinthians 2:9-10 may explain why. It appears that the subject of heaven and what God has ahead for us is so big, so great, so awesome, and so overwhelmingly magnificent that God could only say, "If I painted it, your eye couldn't grasp it all; if I told it, your ear couldn't absorb it all; if I wrote it; your mind couldn't imagine it all."

Often, people who do not listen to what the Holy Spirit is saying, tend to minimize heaven. They think that life here on earth (based on what they have seen, heard, or imagined) is as good as it gets. Their concept of heaven is not very exciting, but rather dull, monotonous and boring; they know nothing of the language, the sounds, the sights, and the realities of heaven.

Our Home (III)

In 1 Corinthians 2:9-10 God is telling us, "Have you seen snow-capped mountains, rushing rivers, white-sand beaches, rain forests, or redwood forests? Have you toured the seven natural wonders of the world? Even if you have seen them all, they cannot begin to describe what your eyes will see in heaven. You will have to see it for yourself, for even if I used every word you can presently understand, or let your imagination explore its farthest boundaries, you would not grasp it. I have sent the Holy Spirit to let you in on some of My secrets; to let you know that it's all true; to assure you that it's better than you think; to fan the flame of your hope; to give you a foretaste of things to come; and to assure you that at my right hand there are pleasures forevermore."

There is no need to be worried by facetious people who try to make the Christian hope of "Heaven" ridiculous by saying they do not want "to spend eternity playing harps". The answer to such people is that if they cannot understand books written for grown-ups, they should not talk about them.

– C. S. LEWIS

He Gives You Peace

"Peace I leave with you, My peace I give to you;
not as the world gives do I give to you. Let not
your heart be troubled, neither let it be afraid."
– John 14:27 –

If you don't have peace about what you are doing, stop doing it.

The peace that God gives you is not circumstantial peace. Being in a hammock at the beach on a warm sunny day is not a picture of God's peace. Remember, the peace in your heart is God's peace; it's there because He's there, not because everything around you is calm and serene.

Christ in You, You in Christ (I)

God alone made it possible for you to be in Christ Jesus.
For our benefit God made Christ to be wisdom itself. He is
the one who made us acceptable to God. He made us pure
and holy, and He gave Himself to purchase our freedom.
– I Corinthians 1:30 NLT –

For it has pleased God to tell His people that
the riches and glory of Christ are for you Gentiles, too.
For this is the secret: Christ lives in you, and this is
your assurance that you will share in His glory.
– Colossians 1:27 NLT –

As a child of God, you are in Christ and He is in you.
Each is significant in the following ways:

Being in Christ means that you receive the benefits of
all that He has done for you through His death, burial,
resurrection and ascension;
Christ being in you means that you receive the benefits
of His presence, character and nature within you.

Being in Christ changes your position before God;
Christ being in you changes the inward condition of
your heart.

Christ in You, You in Christ (II)

Being in Christ opens your eyes to the beauty of God's love;
Christ being in you floods your heart with that same love.

Being in Christ allows you to see what God wants you to become;
Christ being in you means that you can become what God wants you to be.

Being in Christ means that He is the atmosphere in which you live your day;
Christ being in you means that each day His strength is your strength, His peace is your peace, His power is your power, His victory is your victory, His life is your life.

Being in Christ brings you into heavenly realities;
Christ being in you brings heavenly realities into your earthly walk.

In His Time

Be patient, we don't need to know everything right now. In this life we won't be able to resolve every question, solve every problem, or understand every situation. In time, everything will be made clear.

Not every promise of God is intended for now. Some things will be for another time and another season. We don't need to fret over God's timetable. We will inherit all the promises of God through faith and patience.

For we know in part and we prophesy in part.
For now we see in a mirror, dimly, but
then face to face. Now I know in part, but then
I shall know just as I also am known.
– 1 Corinthians 13:9, 12 –

For I consider that the sufferings of this
present time are not worthy to be compared
with the glory which shall be revealed in us.
– Romans 8:18 –

Lean upon Him

You can lean upon the Lord – He is strong enough to keep you from falling, tender enough to keep from despairing, and caring enough to always make you feel welcomed.

As John upon his dear Lord's breast,
So would I lean, so would I rest;
As empty shell in depths of sea,
So would I sink, be filled with Thee.
And so though daily duties crowd,
And dust of earth be like a cloud,
Through noise of words, O Lord, my Rest,
Thy John would lean upon Thy breast.

– AMY CARMICHAEL

The Word of God (I)

Paul tells Timothy, "The word of God is not imprisoned" (2 Tim. 2:9 NASB).

Throughout the centuries God's servants have known imprisonment, been bound by chains, and kept from preaching and teaching the Word of God. The messenger of the Word may be imprisoned by adversaries but the Word of God cannot be.

William Punshon shares these thoughts with us about the Word of God:

> The reasoned cast it into the furnace, which his own negligence had heated "seven times hotter" than its wont – but it came out without the smell of fire. The formalist fastened serpents around it to poison it – but it shook them off and felt no harm. The infidel cast it overboard in a tempest of sophistry and sarcasm – but it rode gallantly upon the crest of the proud waters. And it is living still, yet heard in the loudest swelling of the storm. It has been speaking all the while – it is speaking now.

The Word of God (II)

No one can put a chain around God's words and limit its movement, bind it purpose, chain its influence, weaken its authority, or contain its power.

No warrior can dull the edges of its blade;
  No intellectual can undermine its truth;
No skeptic can lessen its authenticity;
  No mocker can weaken its foundations;
No philosopher can out-think its penetrating insight;
  No strongman can weaken its power;
No religion can replace its transforming power.

The rebellious fight it, the disobedient ignore it, the stubborn refuse it, the indifferent ignore it, the lazy neglect it, the careless skim over it, the foolish despise it, the runaway turns his back on it, and the traitor renounces it.

The hungry one eats it, the weary one rests in it, the traveler finds his way in it, the humble one learns from it, the servant yields to it, the submissive one obeys it, the worshipper loves it, the downcast one is encouraged by it, the weary one is strengthened by it, the sick one is healed by it, and the wise one builds his life upon it.

Perspective

No eye has seen, no ear has heard,
and no mind has imagined what God
has prepared for those who love him.
– 1 Corinthians 2:9 –

"God, everything is changing."
"I'm not."
"People are restless."
"I am in control."
"Things around me are so shaky."
"You are standing on a rock that cannot be moved."
"The economy is unstable."
"I own the cattle on a thousand hills."
"How can I cope?"
"You will always have My grace."
"I am worried."
"Do you believe I care?"
"I wonder if something bad will happen."
"Do you believe I am good?"
"I am afraid."
"Don't you believe that I love you?"
"What will become of me?"
"You can't imagine how wonderful it is going to be!"

Your Good Shepherd

God never leaves His child to fail when in the path of obedience.

— THEODORE CUYLER

Are you where God would have you be? If you are, then be afraid to complain of circumstances which God has ordained on purpose to work out in you the very image and likeness of His Son.

— MARK GUY PEARSE

The Lord is your Shepherd to guide, watch, preserve, restore, and tend, as well as to feed. His eyes never slumber, and His hands never rest. His heart never ceases to beat with love, and His shoulders are never weary of carrying His people's burdens.

— CHARLES H. SPURGEON

November

God Identifies (I)

God identifies:

- with the gardener, for He planted the garden where man first lived;
- with the artist, for He paints every sunrise and sunset;
- with the astronomer, for He placed the moon and sun in the heavens and named all the stars;
- with the writer, for He wrote a book of remembrance, and love letters to His people;
- with the singer, for He joys over His people with singing;
- with the musician, for He places songs and melodies of praise in our hearts;
- with the biologist, for He knows our frame and has knit our parts together;
- with the architect, for He designed the universe and everything that is in it;
- with the physicist; for He sustains and holds all things together;
- with the builder, for He has built many mansions.

God Identifies (II)

God identifies:

- with the doctor, for He is the healer, and life and death are in His hands;
- with the politician, for He rules over all;
- with the rancher, for He owns the cattle on a thousand hills;
- with the accountant, for He records the treasures that are being laid up in heaven;
- with the soldier, for He is the mighty warrior and defender;
- with the traveler, for the clouds are the dust of His feet;
- with the athlete, for He is triumphant over all;
- with the policeman, for He guards and protects His people;
- with the lawyer, for He has said, "Come let us reason together";
- with the philanthropist, for He is the provider of all our needs;
- with the philosopher, for with Him are all the issues of life.

God Identifies (III)

God identifies:

- with the orator, for His voice is as the sound of many waters;
- with the parent, for He is the Father of whom the whole family in heaven and earth is named;
- with the counselor, for He is familiar with all our ways and guides those who follow Him;
- with the pastor, for He has a shepherd's heart and tenderly cares for His sheep;
- with the listener, for He is attentive to our prayers;
- with the devoted, for He has loved us with an everlasting love;
- with the giver, for He freely gives us all things to enjoy;
- with the sufferer, for His Son was a man of sorrows and acquainted with grief;
- with the mourner, for He witnessed the death of His Son upon the cross;
- with the joyful, for He celebrates each time a lost child returns home;
- with the wedding planner, for He has set the date when His Son shall wed His bride.

Dare I ask? Is Jesus Enough?

Do not be anxious about anything ...
present your requests to God.
– Philippians 4:6 NIV –

We all have, in a given moment, a need of the heart. Loneliness is a big need. We can be in a crowd and feel lonely. Is Jesus enough to fill that hole? *"Peace I leave with you; My peace I give you."* (John 14:27 NIV).

Concerning issues of sin: the Holy Spirit may reveal something in our heart that is not right. Anger, hatred, greed. Did Jesus' death on the Cross cover it? *"If we confess our sins, He is faithful and just to forgive us our sins and to cleanse us from all unrighteousness"* (1 John 1:9 NIV).

Concerning a sense of worth. Can it be found in Jesus? *"My frame was not hidden from You when I was made in the secret place ... Your eyes saw my unformed body"* (Ps. 139:15 NIV).

-Char Lessin

Dare I Ask? Is Jesus Enough?

I may feel insecure. Is He enough? *"I have set the Lord always before me. Because He is at my right hand, I will not be shaken"* (Ps. 16:8 NIV).

Worry can be small or huge. Is there an answer? *"Cast all your anxiety on Him because He cares for you"* (1 Peter 5:7 NIV).

Hurt, rejection? Is He enough?
"The Lord is a refuge ... a stronghold in times of trouble. You, O Lord, have never forsaken those who seek You" (Ps. 9:9 & 10 NIV).

Heaviness of heart. Where is Jesus? *"You are my hiding place ... You surround me with songs of deliverance"* (Ps. 32:7 NIV).

"You turned my wailing into dancing You removed my sackcloth and clothed me with joy" (Ps. 30:11 NIV).

-Char Lessin

Dare I Ask? Is Jesus Enough?

Fear of man is a terrible bondage. What do people think? We must be driven by what the Lord thinks, not what man thinks. Knowing we have His approval is our place of rest in all we do. *"And whatever you do, do it heartily, as to the Lord and not to men"* (Col. 3:23 NIV).

"You have made known to me the path of life; You will fill me with joy in Your presence" (Psalm 16:11 NIV).

Contentment – can I be content with what I have, or do I need more? Can I be content in who God made me, or do I have to try to be someone else? *"But godliness with contentment is great gain"* (1 Tim. 6:6 NIV).

What's my address? His Presence! That is where I live.

There are no cracks or imperfections in what He does in our lives. He is about bringing us closer and closer into His heart.

I love the freedom Jesus gives.

Jesus is the Beauty of every day!

-Char Lessin

God's Word Cannot be Broken

All Scripture is God's written Word. It is 100% reliable because God is 100% infallible. Every word in the Scriptures is God-breathed. Every promise that is spoken has come from God's heart, and every truth that is proclaimed is a revelation of God's will.

Every prophecy that is recorded in the Scriptures has been fulfilled or will be fulfilled, not generally, but exactly as it is written, down to the smallest detail.

The Scriptures have endured the test of time – men have tried to destroy them, but they still remain; men have tried to dispute them, but they have had the final say in every argument; men have tried to deny them, but they stand over each man's grave as a living testimony to all that is true, righteous, and eternal.

> *"Heaven and earth shall pass away,*
> *but My words shall not pass away."*
> *– Matthew 24:35 –*

> *"For verily I say unto you, till heaven and*
> *earth pass, one jot or one tittle shall in no wise*
> *pass from the law, till all be fulfilled."*
> *– Matthew 5:18 KJV –*

You Belong to a Kingdom that Will Last Forever

Since we are receiving a Kingdom that is
unshakable, let us be thankful and please God
by worshiping Him with holy fear and awe.
– Hebrews 12:28 NLT –

You are living in a world that is temporary, but you are living for the things that are eternal. Every system or power that has man as its source will eventually falter, fail, and fade from view. Throughout history kings have been overthrown, leaders have fallen from power, armies have been defeated, riches have been depleted, and fortresses have been toppled.

There is no secure place around us where the insecure can find a haven. It is only in the kingdom of God that anyone can find true rest and security. No rebellion can overthrow God's kingdom, no weapon can penetrate its defenses, and no warrior can dethrone its King.

Everything about the kingdom of God is solid, sure, and steady. It is reliable, dependable, and impenetrable. The kingdom of God is eternal. It is the only Kingdom that will remain. The way of the Kingdom is where your feet can walk; the truth of the Kingdom is why your faith can soar; the love of the Kingdom is what your heart can fully embrace.

The New Covenant (I)

*You have come to Mount Zion and to the city of
the living God, the heavenly Jerusalem, to an
innumerable company of angels, to the general
assembly and church of the firstborn who are registered
in heaven, to God the Judge of all, to the spirits of
just men made perfect, to Jesus the Mediator of the
new covenant, and to the blood of sprinkling
that speaks better things than that of Abel.*
– Hebrews 12:22-24 –

The New Covenant is a covenant that has been sealed by
God's promise and His oath. It is an eternal agreement
that God has made with you through His Son. He sent
Him from heaven to earth to establish this covenant
with you. The New Covenant is a covenant of grace,
making available to you what you could never deserve
or earn.

What was incomplete in the Old Covenant became
perfect in the new; what was temporary in the Old
Covenant became permanent in the new; what was
insufficient in the Old Covenant became a completed
work in the new. The blood covenant of Jesus Christ
perfected the work of your salvation.

The New Covenant (II)

*Now may the God of peace who brought up our
Lord Jesus from the dead, that great Shepherd
of the sheep, through the blood of the everlasting
covenant, make you complete in every good
work to do His will, working in you what is well
pleasing in His sight, through Jesus Christ,
to whom be glory forever and ever. Amen.*
– Hebrews 13:20-21 –

When Jesus came, He came to save you, cleanse you, forgive you, and deliver you from your sins. He lived a sinless life so that He could offer Himself upon the cross as your substitute. He was the sacrificial lamb who made atonement for your sin.

The blood of Jesus cleanses you and claims you. You have been bought with the blood of Christ. He is your Redeemer and He has taken full responsibility for your life. The shed blood of Jesus means that your past is forgiven and your present and your future are with Him. The loudest message of the New Covenant is, "I love you, I have bought you and you are mine."

You Have All You Need

Wherefore take unto you the whole armour of God.
– Ephesians 6:13 KJV –

The grace of God covers you, the presence of God is in you, the angels of God are with you, the arms of God are around you, the gifts of God are for you, and the power of God is upon you. He has not abandoned you or left you in this world as an orphan, alone and forsaken.

He has called you to serve Him and equipped you to serve Him. He has given you the ministry of reconciliation so that you can reach out to others. He has given you the ministry of intercession so that you can pray for others. He has given you the ministry of hope so that you can comfort others.

You are His ambassador on a holy assignment. God is for you, the Holy Spirit is in you, Jesus is with you, and all the heavenly hosts are on your side. The weapons of your warfare are mighty through God to the pulling down of strongholds. He has given you the whole armor of God for every battle you face. He has you covered from head to toe.

Jesus Is Coming Back

Jesus Christ is coming back. The outcome of all things has already been determined. Jesus is the winner. He is without rival in the universe. No evil doer, no outlaw, no terrorist, no anarchist will be standing in the end. Every enemy of God will be defeated, every false prophet will be exposed, every evil spirit will be chained, and every accusing tongue will be silenced.

The final chapter of history has already been written, and there will be no need for rewrites or revisions. God's plan will be fulfilled. There will be a new heaven and a new earth. One day soon, you will forever be with the Lord.

Maranatha!

And they speak of how you are looking forward to the coming of God's Son from heaven – Jesus, whom God raised from the dead. He is the one who has rescued us from the terrors of the coming judgment.
– 1 Thessalonians 1:10 NLT –

For the Lord Himself shall descend from heaven with a shout, with the voice of the archangel, and with the trump of God.
– 1 Thessalonians 4:16 KJV –

God Will Not Fail You (I)

You are God's child and He is your Father. He loves and cares for you more than you will ever know. He is the One who sent His Son to die for you. He is the One who ran to receive you when He saw your heart turn to Him for forgiveness. He is the One whose pleasure it is to give you the Kingdom. All that He is, He is for you. All His redemptive names are yours to claim and call upon.

He is Jehovah-Jireh, the God who provides for you;
He is Jehovah-Rapha, the God who heals you;
He is Jehovah-Nissi, the God who is your banner;
He is Jehovah-M'Kaddesh, the God who sanctifies you;
He is Jehovah-Shalom, the God who is your peace;
He is Jehovah-Tsidkenu, the God who is your righteousness;
He is Jehovah-Rohi, the God who is your shepherd;
He is Jehovah-Shammah, the God who is present with you.

God Will Not Fail You (II)

Let your conversation be without covetousness;
and be content with such things as ye have: for He
hath said, I will never leave thee, nor forsake thee.
So that we may boldly say, The Lord is my helper,
and I will not fear what man shall do unto me.
– Hebrews 13:5-6 KJV –

The depth of His love for you cannot be measured, and its height cannot be scaled. He wants you to trust Him completely because He will not fail you. He cannot. When you go through trials He will keep you from defeat, when you face temptations He will keep from shame. When the enemy comes in like a flood, He will raise up a standard against Him. No weapon that is formed against you will prosper, for the battle is the Lord's. You will never face an enemy that you have to fear or run from, for "greater is He that is in you than he that is in the world." You life belongs to Him and your times are in His hands.

Jesus Will Never Let You Go (I)

*[For it is He] Who rescued and saved us from
such a perilous death, and He will still rescue and
save us; in and on Him we have set our hope (our joyful
and confident expectation) that He will again deliver us
[from danger and destruction and draw us to Himself].*
– 2 Corinthians 1:10 AMP –

Jesus is with you always. No one can pluck you out of His hand.

He is in you and you are in Him. He is your Shepherd and He will watch over you. You need not fear any evil. He is your High Priest. He is daily interceding for you and His prayers are being answered. He is your Bridegroom. He is preparing a place for you in His Father's house and He will come for you.

His hands that hold you are pierced hands. If you ever question His love for you, look at His hands. His arms were once outstretched on the cross so that He could embrace you now with His unfailing love.

When He shed His blood He took your sin; when He died on the cross He took your death; when He ascended into hell He took your judgment; when He rose from the grave He won your victory.

Jesus Will Never Let You Go (II)

Jesus will never ask you to do something without His grace. In the dark times He will be your light. In troubled times He will be your security. In uncertain times He will be your guidance. In fearful times He will be your peace. You will never face a day without Him; you will never take a step without Him walking beside you; you will never face a need without His supply; you will never face a circumstance that He can't bring you through triumphantly.

Our response to Jesus should be "Yes" to Him and His Word; a response that says "No" to fear and darkness; a response of hope that moves us ahead in the confidence of knowing that the best is yet to be. A response of praise and worship for the wisdom of His ways, the beauty of His character, and the blessings of His goodness that He has showered upon us in Christ. A response of obedience that follows the Lord wherever He leads, that reaches out to those in need, that seeks His honor and glory. And a response that finds us being faithful in the thing He has called us to do until He comes.

One Plus God Is a Majority

But without faith it is impossible to please Him, for He
who comes to God must believe that He is, and that
He is a rewarder of those who diligently seek Him.
– Hebrews 11:6 KJV –

Factor God into everything you do, into every circumstance of life, and into every decision you make.

Take "I can't" out of your vocabulary and replace it with
    "God can".
Replace "I am nothing" with
    "He is everything".
Exchange "I am inadequate" with
    "He is sufficient".
Substitute "I fall short" with
    "He abounds".
Put off "I am too limited" and put on
    "He is more than enough".

Destiny

*For now we are looking in a mirror that gives only
a dim (blurred) reflection [of reality as in a riddle or
enigma], but then [when perfection comes] we shall
see in reality and face to face! Now I know in part
(imperfectly), but then I shall know and understand
fully and clearly, even in the same manner as I have been
fully and clearly known and understood [by God].*
– 1 Corinthians 13:12 AMP –

It is good to walk the path of a pilgrim;
　　it is better to arrive at your glorious destination.
It is good to live the life of faith;
　　it is better to receive faith's final reward.
It is good to overcome and persevere;
　　it is better to wear the victor's crown.
It is good to live for Jesus day by day;
　　it is better to see Him face to face.

Your Highest Purpose

*[For my determined purpose is] that I may
know Him [that I may progressively become more
deeply and intimately acquainted with Him,
perceiving and recognizing and understanding
the wonders of His Person more strongly and more
clearly], and that I may in that same way come to
know the power outflowing from His resurrection
[which it exerts over believers], and that I may so share
His sufferings as to be continually transformed [in
spirit into His likeness even] to His death.*
– Philippians 3:10 AMP –

Your highest purpose is:

- To know the GOD who formed you;
- To yield to HIS ARMS that draw you;
- To hear HIS VOICE that calls you;
- To follow HIS WILL that guides you;
- To trust HIS GRACE that keeps you;
- To seek HIS HEART that loves you.

Both Sides Now

Jesus is the Servant and the Master,
    the Lamb and the Shepherd,
the Giver and the Gift,
    the Counselor and the Counsel,
the Way and the Destination,
    the Sacrifice and the High Priest,
the Teacher and the Truth,
    the Vine and the Fruit,
the Author and the Story,
    the Physician and the Cure,
the Cornerstone and the Foundation,
    the Lifeline and the Anchor,
the Promise and the Fulfillment,
    the Warrior and the Armor,
the Prophet and the Prophecy,
    the Beginning and the End.

The Pot and the Potter

We now have this light shining in our hearts,
but we ourselves are like fragile clay jars containing
this great treasure. This makes it clear that our great
power is from God, not from ourselves.
– 2 Corinthians 4:7 NLT –

The clay pot said, "I feel so useless."
The Potter said, "I made you for My special purpose."

The clay pot said, "I am so common looking."
The Potter said, "It is what you are in My hands that makes you beautiful."

The clay pot said, "How can I be used, for I have a crack?"
The Potter said, "Cracks may come, but My skillful hands will restore you, and I will keep you from ever being shattered."

The clay pot said, "I have nothing to offer!"
The Potter said, "It is what I put within you that will make all the difference."

The Voice of the Lord (I)

His voice was like the sound of many waters.
– Revelation 1:15 –

God speaks. His voice is as loud as thunder and as soft as a whisper. His voice is recognizable to His children and as clear as a pure mountain stream. His voice is as soothing as the words of a mother speaking comfort to her hurting child; as assuring as the words of a father speaking courage to a fearful child.

God's voice is like the sound of no other. It is a peaceful voice (Ps. 85:8), a healing voice (Ps. 107:20), a seeking voice (Gen. 3:9), a merciful voice (Num. 7:89), a majestic voice (Ps. 29:4), a calling voice (Isa. 6:8), an affirming voice (Matt. 3:17), a great voice (Rev. 1:10). We need to seek His voice, listen to His voice, respond to His voice, follow His voice, and trust His voice.

We do not need to avoid or fear the voice of God. Everything He has to say to us is true, is good, is loving, and is life giving. When His words are found we can eat them, for they are the joy and rejoicing of our hearts (Jer. 15:16).

The Voice of the Lord (II)

C. S. Lewis shares the following experience his wife had in being reluctant to listen to God's voice:

> She was haunted all one morning as she went about her work with the obscure sense of God (so to speak) 'at her elbow,' demanding her attention. And of course, not being a perfected saint, she had the feeling that it would be a question, as it usually is, of some unrepented sin or tedious duty. At last she gave in – I know one puts it off – and faced Him. But the message was, 'I want to give you something' and instantly she entered into joy.

When God spoke with Abraham He said, "I am your exceeding great reward" (Gen. 15:1). Now that is the best thing anyone could ever hear. You need to hear that deep within your spirit today. You need to hear God speak to you. Put out all other sounds, all other noises, all other voices. Listen to Him as He says, "You are My child. You are Mine and I give Myself to you."

He Fully Met Our Needs

*For when we were still without strength,
in due time Christ died for the ungodly. For scarcely
for a righteous man will one die; yet perhaps for a
good man someone would even dare to die. But God
demonstrates His own love toward us, in that while
we were still sinners, Christ died for us.*

– Romans 5:6-8 –

Jesus didn't leave heaven because He was in need of a Savior. He didn't fulfill the law because He was waiting for the Messiah. He didn't die on the cross because He was guilty of sin. He didn't rise from the dead because He was in need of hope. He didn't become a High Priest because He was in need of prayer. He didn't send the Holy Spirit because He was in need of the comforter. He did it all because we were the ones in need of all He came to do!

God's Overwhelming Generosity

For you are becoming progressively acquainted with and recognizing more strongly and clearly the grace of our Lord Jesus Christ (His kindness, His gracious generosity, His undeserved favor and spiritual blessing), [in] that though He was [so very] rich, yet for your sakes He became [so very] poor, in order that by His poverty you might become enriched (abundantly supplied).

– 2 Corinthians 8:9 AMP –

Everything in your life that flows out of love has come to you from God. Everything in your life that is good has been initiated by God. God has done everything for you, He is everything to you, and He is enriching other lives through you. His generosity is overwhelming; His blessings are limitless; His love is endless.

᾿ No one has favored you more than God. He has removed every stain of your sin, He has cleansed all the defilement of your iniquity, and He has silenced every voice of condemnation that hung over your head. He has saved you, redeemed you, and justified you.

God's Overwhelming Graciousness

*For you are becoming progressively acquainted
with and recognizing more strongly and clearly the grace
of our Lord Jesus Christ (His kindness, His **gracious**
generosity, His undeserved favor and spiritual blessing),
[in] that though He was [so very] rich, yet for your sakes
He became [so very] poor, in order that by His poverty
you might become enriched (abundantly supplied).*
– 2 Corinthians 8:9 AMP –

All of God's grace abounds toward you, all of Christ's riches are made available to you, and all spiritual blessings are provided for you.

In Christ, you have received the treasures that can never be taken away, the hope that can never fade away, and the life that will never pass away.

God's Overwhelming Riches

*For you are becoming progressively acquainted
with and recognizing more strongly and clearly the grace
of our Lord Jesus Christ (His kindness, His gracious
generosity, His undeserved favor and spiritual blessing),
[in] that though He was [so very] rich, yet for your sakes
He became [so very] poor, in order that by His poverty
you might become enriched (abundantly supplied).*
– 2 Corinthians 8:9 AMP –

As you walk with Jesus day by day, you will find that your thankfulness to Him is an ever-increasing symphony of praise, building into a lifelong crescendo of gratitude that flows from your heart to His. You, who have so little, have received so much, because He has been so generous.

There are so many riches that He has given to you; so many answers to prayer that He has granted to you; so many kindnesses that He has manifested to you; so many joys that He has provided for you; so many mercies that He has extended to you; so many benefits that He has showered upon you. Everything you have has come from Him, and that is the reason why your heart can be so grateful.

Move On in Me

There is more to drink than what you've tasted,
    Move on in Me.
There are more vistas to discover than what you've seen,
    Move on in Me.
There is more to feast upon than what you've eaten,
    Move on in Me.
There are more heights to climb than what you've conquered,
    Move on in Me.
There is more grace to receive than what you've been given,
    Move on in Me.
There are more joys to delight in than what you've enjoyed,
    Move on in Me.
There is more love to embrace than what you've experienced,
    Move on in Me.
There are more blessings to come than what you've received,
    Move on in Me.

You Are Loved

*The LORD has appeared of old to me, saying: "Yes,
I have loved you with an everlasting love; therefore
with lovingkindness I have drawn you."*
– Jeremiah 31:3 –

Jesus loves you,
    no one could be kinder;
He cares for you,
    no one could be more thoughtful;
He prays for you,
    no one could be more understanding;
He guides you,
    no one could more watchful;
He keeps you,
    no one could be more protective.

As you live in the light of Jesus' love, He wants you to
"press on" in your daily walk of faith and obedience,
and to "press in" to all that He has in His heart for you.

Faith

What is faith? It is the confident assurance that
what we hope for is going to happen. It is the evidence
of things we cannot yet see. So, you see, it is impossible
to please God without faith. Anyone who wants to
come to Him must believe that there is a God and
that He rewards those who sincerely seek Him.
– Hebrews 11:1, 6 NLT –

What things are possible for you today through faith? All things are possible, because your faith is in the God who knows no impossibilities.

When the things that you are experiencing don't make sense, faith says, "God knows what He is doing."

When your resources don't match your need, faith says, "God is my provider."

When you are fearful to take the next step, faith says, "God will not fail me."

When you're not sure what to do next, faith says, "God will guide me."

When you are in a situation that seems impossible, faith says, "Nothing is too hard for the Lord."

December

The School of the Holy Spirit

"The Holy Spirit ... He will teach you everything
and will remind you of everything I have told you."
– John 14:26 NLT –

The moment you gave your life to Christ He enrolled you in His school. Your teacher is the Holy Spirit and life is your classroom. He has surrounded you with lots of fellow students, but you will always have His personal and undivided attention. When Jesus enrolled you in His school He placed you there for a lifetime. Heaven is your graduation. Until that day, you will always be taught by the Holy Spirit and have new lessons to learn.

Today, in your life, in your circumstances, in your relationships, in your trials, in your pain, in your persecutions, Jesus has things for you to learn. The Holy Spirit is teaching and instructing you in His ways, His working, and in His wisdom. He is teaching you about the kingdom of God, about the heart of God, and about the plan and purposes of God for your life.

Learn Your Lessons Well

What is the Holy Spirit teaching you today? What words of Jesus is the Holy Spirit bringing to your remembrance? What step of obedience does He want you to take? What word of faith does He want you to trust? Paul tells us that he had learned to be content in whatever state he was in – whether he had much or little. The Holy Spirit used the circumstances in Paul's life, the times of plenty and the times of lack, to teach Paul contentment. In every situation of life, the Holy Spirit has something new to teach us. Remain teachable.

I always say to my children that no matter how many mistakes we make or how tough it gets, as long as we have learned a lesson from it, no experience is wasted ... thank God for every situation that you are in because He is teaching you lessons you will never forget.

– ANGUS BUCHAN

Attitudes (I)

Pride asks: "How will it make me look?"
  Greed asks: "What can I get out of it?"
Indifference asks: "Why should I bother?"
  Selfishness asks: "What about me?"

The Cross of Jesus Christ puts to death the following attitudes:

SPITE "See, I told you so."
  REBELLION "I want my own way."
IMPATIENCE "I want it now!"
  CONTEMPT "Who do you think you are!"
PRIDE "You can't treat me that way!"
  REVENGE "I'll get even."
DEFIANCE "You can't tell me what to do."
  SELFISHNESS "I did it my way."

Attitudes (II)

Heart attitudes of the Kingdom:

- "How may I serve you?"
- "I will wait for God's time."
- "I will not carry a grudge."
- "I am not my own."
- "This job is not beneath me."
- "I extend mercy instead of judgment."
- "I honor you."
- "Will this please the Lord?"
- "By the grace of God I am what I am."
- "Thy will be done."
- "I did it God's way."

Obedience is the opener of eyes.

– GEORGE MACDONALD

Psalm 37:4

*Delight yourself in the Lord, and He
shall give you the desires of your heart.*

Continue to be soft and pliable in the Lord's hands and out of that relationship will come the things that define you at the deepest level of your heart – revealing to yourself and others what you are really about – what moves you, motivates you, and forms your true longings. These longings come from God's heart touching yours – resulting in the things that He will work in you and bring to pass through your life. (Based upon Psalm 37:4)

The Invitation

Take His salvation and RECEIVE HIM.
"As many as received Him, to them gave He power to become the sons of God, even to them that believe on His name" (John 1:12 KJV).

Take His call and SEEK HIM.
"When You said, "Seek My face," my heart said to You, "Your face, Lord, I will seek" (Psalm 27:8).

Take His yoke and JOIN HIM.
"My yoke is easy and My burden is light" (Matt. 11:30).

Take His name and HONOR HIM.
"You are worthy, O Lord, to receive glory and honor and power" (Rev. 4:11).

Take His word and KNOW HIM.
"That I may know Him and the power of His resurrection" (Phil. 3:10).

Take His promises and TRUST HIM.
"Trust in the Lord, and do good; dwell in the land, and feed on His faithfulness" (Ps. 37:3).

Puffed Up or Built Up? (I)

Mere knowledge causes people to be puffed up (to bear themselves loftily and be proud), but love (affection and goodwill and benevolence) edifies and builds up and encourages one to grow [to his full stature].
– 1 Corinthians 8:1 AMP –

The Scriptures present to us many contrasts. The Word of God not only unites but it also divides. It separates light from darkness, truth from error, sin from righteousness, flesh from Spirit, the carnal mind from the spiritual mind, the old man from the new man, the world from the kingdom of God, life from death, idolatry from true worship, a believer from an unbeliever, and Christ from the devil. All of these are examples of how the Word of God separates and divides.

The Scripture in 1 Corinthians 8:1 also makes a clear distinction between what puffs us up and what builds us up. The work and ministry of the Holy Spirit in our lives is always to build us up and never to puff us up. The purpose of teaching, preaching, or ministering in the body of Christ is for the purpose of building believers up in Christ, not puffing them up in the flesh.

Puffed Up or Built Up? (II)

*I have been crucified with Christ [in Him I have
shared His crucifixion]; it is no longer I who live,
but Christ (the Messiah) lives in me; and the life I
now live in the body I live by faith in (by adherence to
and reliance on and complete trust in) the Son of
God, Who loved me and gave Himself up for me.*
– Galatians 2:20 AMP –

The natural man (the flesh) loves to be puffed up. It
glories in its accomplishments, its knowledge, its status,
its position, and its talents. It seeks out and welcomes
all forms of recognition, flattery, and applause.

Why would Paul glory in the cross when it put to
death all the glory he could receive from the world and
no longer allowed him to be puffed up by the accomplishments of his flesh? Paul gloried in the cross because
it brought him into the life that can only be found in
Christ. Paul saw, through the work of the cross, how
good it was to be delivered from the bondage of promot-
ing himself, to enjoying the freedom of knowing Christ.
He sums up this glorious freedom when he writes.

Puffed Up or Built Up? (III)

Today, it is the will of God for you to be built up in Christ. How does the Holy Spirit build you up? He doesn't build you up by telling you how great you are. He doesn't cater to your ego, your pride, or your flesh. He builds you up by pointing you to Jesus, by strengthening your faith, by sanctifying your spirit, by encouraging you to trust in the Lord with all your heart, by prompting you to take new steps of obedience to the Father's will, by giving you grace, and by extending new mercies every morning.

He builds you up with love, with hope, with truth, with righteousness, with peace, and with joy. He builds you up with the promises of God, with the resurrection of Christ, with the fellowship of believers, with the power of the Kingdom, and with the hope of His calling. He builds you up by assuring you that He is near, by giving you His comfort, by conforming you to the image of Jesus, and by bearing witness to your heart that you belong to the Lord.

Your King and Father

Thou art coming to a King.
Large petitions with thee bring;
For His grace and pow'r are such
None can ever ask too much.

– JOHN NEWTON

If it can be proved that the great Father ever allows any of His children to cry to Him in vain, or if it can be shown that He leaves any of them to stumble home in the dark as best they can, then Christianity has broken down. But can it? There is no cause for alarm ... each child finds a place of his own, and his voice is loved and listened to. It is inconceivable that the Father of fatherhood will overlook one of His children.

– F. W. BOREHAM

The Work Jesus Came to Do (I)

A flawless work – it is without error or mistake.
After He had offered one sacrifice for sins forever, sat down at the right hand of God (Heb. 10:12).

A final work – it will never need to be repeated.
This He did once for all when He offered up Himself (Heb. 7:27).

A finished work – it needs nothing added to make it complete.
Jesus said, "It is finished." With that, He bowed His head and gave up His spirit (John 19:30).

A faithful work–it fulfilled our need for reconciliation with God.
Now all things are of God, who has reconciled us to Himself through Jesus Christ, and has given us the ministry of reconciliation, that is, that God was in Christ reconciling the world to Himself, not imputing their trespasses to them (2 Cor. 5:18-19).

The Work Jesus Came to Do (II)

A freeing work – it delivers us from the penalty and the power of sin.
"Thou shalt call His name JESUS: for He shall save His people from their sins" (Matt. 1:21).

A fruitful work – it brings to us the transforming gift of new life.
Therefore, if anyone is in Christ, he is a new creation; old things have passed away; behold, all things have become new (2 Cor. 5:17).

A fulfilling work – it allows us to serve the living God.
How much more shall the blood of Christ, who through the eternal Spirit offered himself without spot to God, purge your conscience from dead works to serve the living God? (Heb. 9:14).

A forever work – it brings the salvation that will last forever.
He is able to save forever those who draw near to God through Him (Heb. 7:25).

Anointing and Talent

Now He who establishes us with you in
Christ and has anointed us is God.
– 2 Corinthians 1:21 –

When someone sings and you are caught up with the beauty of the singer's voice, that is talent; when someone sings and you are caught up with the beauty of the Lord, that is anointing.

When someone writes and stirs your imagination, that is talent; when someone writes and stirs your heart, that is anointing.

When someone speaks and gets you to follow him, that is talent; when someone speaks and gets you to follow Jesus, that is anointing.

When someone motivates you to take up a noble cause, that is talent; when someone motivates you to take up your cross, that is anointing.

When you are filled with self-confidence and achieve your goals, that is talent; when you are filled with the Holy Spirit and do the will of God, that is anointing.

When you work hard and receive the applause of men, that is talent; when you remain faithful and receive the approval of God, that is anointing.

May You Be Blessed

"God shall bless us; and all the ends
of the earth shall fear Him"
– Psalm 67:7 KJV –

May you be blessed with:

- Comfort as you mourn;
- Peace when you are troubled;
- Grace when you are needy;
- Courage when are afraid;
- Strength when you are weary;
- Faith when you are doubting;
- Hope when you are uncertain;
- Tenderness when you need to be assured;
- Wisdom when you need to know the way.

Waiting for God's Time (I)

"Rest in the LORD, and wait patiently for Him."
– Psalm 37:7 –

One of the ancient meanings of the word "wait" is "to bind together by twisting." Binding cords together by hand takes time. It is a process with a purpose that takes patience. God, like a master weaver, does a creative work within us during the waiting times in our lives. It is during our waiting times that God binds our lives with His, as a rope-maker binds together threads of twine. When this happens we experience the stretching of our faith and the testing of our patience.

As He works, He strengthens us and pulls us closer to His heart. He does this because He desires intimacy with us. Before He gives us what we are waiting for, He wants to give us more of Himself. In the waiting times we are strengthened with His strength, and the fiber of His character is worked within us.

Waiting for God's Time (II)

"Let none that wait on Thee be ashamed."
– Psalm 25:3 KJV –

It is important to understand that waiting times are not times of denial but are times of preparation. When it is God's time to bring something into our lives, He will often do it after He has prepared us to receive it.

God may withhold an overflow of finances until He has taught us how to give. He may withhold a place of leadership until He has taught us how to serve. He may withhold honor until He has taught us humility. He may withhold possessions until He has taught us contentment. He may withhold a relationship until He has taught us to be complete in Him. He may withhold an active ministry until He has taught us how to be still. He may withhold guidance until He has taught us what is pleasing in His sight.

Waiting for God's Time (III)

*"Let integrity and uprightness
preserve me; for I wait on Thee."*
– Psalm 25:21 KJV –

Another aspect of waiting is expectation. Our waiting times are not meant to be times of heaviness and drudgery. Expectation is like the wind blowing away the clouds that would try to settle over our souls. A man once built his home on a high hill. His back porch faced east. Each morning he would awake an hour before sunrise. He would shower, make himself a cup of coffee, and sit on his favorite rocking chair out on the back porch. In the darkness, he would quietly wait with expectation for the sun to come up and cast its brilliant, golden light across the landscape. Faith is our back porch rocking chair. In it we rest with expectation for the light of God's promises to dawn upon us. Faith keeps our heads lifted, our eyes focused, and our purpose clear.

Waiting for God's Time (IV)

"Who is among you that feareth the Lord, that obeyeth the voice of His servant, that walketh in darkness, and hath no light? Let him trust in the name of the Lord, and stay upon his God."
– Isaiah 50:10 KJV –

In faith, Abraham waited with expectation for Isaac to be born to Sarah. Isaac, when he was a young man, waited with expectation for his father's servant to return from a distant land with a promised bride. Rebecca waited with expectation during her long journey that brought her to the man she would marry but had never seen.

During our waiting times, expectation helps to keep us spiritually moving ahead instead of becoming passive and indifferent. Expectation moves us from twiddling our thumbs to exercising our faith.

Expectation is what keeps the fisherman coming back to the river in search of a trophy trout. It is what keeps a gold miner panning as he looks for nuggets. It is what keeps the mountain climber going as he anticipates the view that awaits him at the summit. It is what keeps the farmer planting seeds in the springtime as he awaits the summer's harvest.

Waiting for God's Time (V)

"I wait for the Lord, my soul doth wait,
and in His word do I hope."
– Psalm 130:5 kjv –

Waiting times are also times for gathering things together. As we gather, we look at what God is teaching us and revealing to our hearts.

We gather together our thoughts and weigh them against the truth of God's word. We gather together our feelings and make sure they are not taking us in a wrong direction. We gather together our desires and make sure we are not trying to force God's timing.

In our waiting times we are also to gather together our remembrances. God wants us to be filled with memories of His goodness.

We are to gather together the times when God has been faithful to us in our needs, when He has kept us from falling during times of temptation, and when He has comforted us in our trials. He also wants us to remember the times when He has blessed us with favor, when He has smiled upon us and been gracious to us, and when He has brought us unexpected joys. He wants us to remember that He will continue to be to us in the future all that He has been to us in the past.

Waiting for God's Time (VI)

"They that wait upon the LORD shall renew their strength;
they shall mount up with wings as eagles; they shall run,
and not be weary; and they shall walk, and not faint."
– Isaiah 40:31 KJV –

Waiting times are also times for soaring. God wants us to be like the eagle, not like the creatures that live in tunnels or caves. From the caves we develop a human point of view toward our waiting times – a point of view that feeds cynicism, skepticism, and doubt. From the skies we develop a heavenly point of view – a view that feeds faith, confidence, and praise.

We can fly in our waiting times because our wings are the wings of faith, and the promises of God are the winds that give us lift. We don't strive to fly; we simply extend our wings of faith, move them in quiet steps of obedience, and allow the winds of God's promises to send us soaring.

Glory (I)

In John 1:14 we read, "And the Word became flesh, and dwelt among us, and we beheld His glory, glory as of the only begotten from the Father, full of grace and truth."

Have you wondered why the disciples left their all to follow Jesus? What was it about Him that would cause them to take such a drastic step? I think John gives a clue when he tells us, "And we beheld His glory." It seems that in their first encounter with Jesus, God gave the disciples their first glimpse of His glory.

It certainly was not the full revelation of His glory, but it was enough to win their hearts. They heard something in His voice, they saw something in His countenance, and they felt something from His spirit that allowed them to behold Him for the very first time. It was enough to keep them in awe, to keep them in wonder, and keep them desiring to behold Him more and more.

Glory (II)

What is glory? In Hebrew it means splendor, honor, beauty, majesty, grandeur, or excellence. In Greek it means dignity, honor, praise, or esteem. No amount of words, however descriptive they may be, can help us fully grasp what glory truly is. The reason is because glory is not so much about what we describe, as it is about what we behold.

John wasn't given a divine description of Jesus Christ, he was given a personal revelation of Him. John's eyes looked upon the fullness of God's glory – grace and truth in the face of Jesus Christ.

Think of it, Jesus Christ came so that you could behold His glory. Not just a glimpse of His glory, but the fullness of His glory. As we grow in our relationship with Jesus Christ from day to day, we go from glory to glory. We see more of His beauty, learn more of His ways, and understand more of His heart. In many ways, we are like people watching sunbeams coming through the window of our heart – the sunbeams are real and delightful to look upon – but they are nothing compared to the full glory of the sun from which they emanate.

Glory (III)

What is the glory of God? Jesus Christ! Who is the glory of God? Jesus Christ! Where is the glory of God? Jesus Christ. Jesus Christ is the center point, the starting point, and the ending point of the glory of God. We behold the glory of God in the face of Jesus Christ, not somewhere else or through something else.

Signs and wonders are expressions of God's glory, but signs and wonders are not His glory; the heavens declare the glory of God, but the heavens are not His glory; the earth is filled with the glory of God, but the earth is not His glory – Christ, and Christ alone is the glory of God.

Now unto Him that is able to keep you from falling, and to present you faultless before the presence of His glory with exceeding joy.
– Jude 1:24 KJV –

(Jesus Christ) being the brightness of His glory and the express image of His person.
– Hebrews 1:3 –

Glory (IV)

*Father, I desire that they also whom You have
entrusted to Me [as Your gift to Me] may be with
Me where I am, so that they may see My glory, which
You have given Me [Your love gift to Me]; for
You loved Me before the foundation of the world.*
– *John 17:24* AMP –

Jesus wants you to be where He is. Why does He want you to be with Him? One of the greatest cries of His heart was that He wanted you to be with Him so that you could see and know (behold) His glory.

The glory that Jesus now carries in the heavens is beyond anything you have ever seen or known upon this earth. It is a glory that is greater than all the national parks and earthly wonders of the world put together. His glory is more majestic than ascending the heights of the highest mountain peaks; more magnificent than seeing all the world's waterfalls cascading down around you; more glorious than smelling the fragrance of a million roses placed within your grasp; more wondrous than hearing, in the richest and purest tones, the music of the most beautiful symphonies ever composed.

Glory (V)

*And the city had no need of the sun, neither
of the moon, to shine in it: for the glory of God
did lighten it, and the Lamb is the light thereof.*
– Revelation 21:23 KJV –

Jesus wants you to behold His glory for the sheer pleasure of it, for the pure of joy of it, for the absolute delight
of it all. His glory is so great, so vast, and so magnificent
that it will take you an eternity to behold it – a billion,
trillion years to begin to see it, feel it, know it, and experience it. His glory will keep on delighting you, over
and over again. It will be one continuous "Wow, Jesus,
Wow!" forever, and ever, and ever. Hallelujah!

God's True Light

For God Who said, Let light shine out of darkness,
has shone in our hearts so as [to beam forth] the Light
for the illumination of the knowledge of the majesty
and glory of God [as it is manifest in the Person and
is revealed] in the face of Jesus Christ (the Messiah).
– 2 Corinthians 4:6 AMP –

God still guides seeking hearts to the One True Light.
As the world around us grows darker, the Light of Jesus
Christ shines even brighter. He is the Light of truth, of
hope, of purity, and of beauty. His Light shines through
the faces of those who know Him, through the eyes of
those who see Him, through the character of those who
walk with Him, and through the hearts of those who
love Him.

There's No One Like Jesus

For we ourselves have heard Him and we know that
this is indeed the Christ, the Savior of the world.
– John 4:42 –

Jesus lived like no man has ever lived. His obedience was clothed with joy, His motives were bathed in love, His choices were covered with grace.

When Jesus spoke, He spoke as no man had ever spoken. He spoke with authority. His words went deeper than the mind, His words reached the soul, pierced the heart, touched the conscience, and stirred the spirit. What He said could be trusted, and every heart that trusted what He said was changed forever.

When Jesus worked, He worked as no man had ever worked. When He found the sick He showed them the way to healing, when we found the impure He showed them the way to cleansing, when He found the broken He showed them the way to wholeness, when He found the heavy of heart He led them to the fountains of joy, when He found those in darkness He led them to His marvelous light, when He found the thirsty He led them to the rivers of life.

Jesus, What a Wonderful Savior

*"Those the Father has given Me will come
to Me, and I will never reject them."*
– John 6:37 NLT –

The rivers that Jesus wants us to drink from are pure waters, the garments He wants us to wear are spotless, and the road He wants us to travel is the hi-way of holiness. To the sick He reaches out in healing, to the hungry He reaches out with bread, and to the guilty He reaches out with forgiveness. He reaches out to the children and draws them close to His heart. He reaches out to the fearful and gives them peace, and He calms the troubled seas of the oppressed. He reaches out to the broken-hearted and binds their wounds, and He gives liberty to those who are captives. He reaches out with comfort to those who wept, and He prays for those who need strength. He reaches out to the discouraged and gives them hope, and He reaches down to those in despair and places their feet upon the rock of His salvation.

Just As God Has Said

*"Praising God for all the things they had heard
and seen, just as it had been told them."*
– Luke 2:20 –

What the shepherds discovered about God's word is what each of us must discover in our walk with Him. God's level of communication is 100% accurate and reliable. When God speaks His words they are sure and certain. He never uses fill-in words, empty words, or misleading words. His will, His power, and His wisdom are behind everything He says. God doesn't overstate or understate anything. He never embellishes anything. What the shepherds heard was what the shepherds saw and experienced, down to the smallest detail.

What is God saying to you? What do you hear coming from His heart to yours? What promise from His word has He quickened to your spirit? What direction is He leading you to go? What step of faith is He asking to take? If the Shepherds hadn't stepped out on His word and gone to Bethlehem they never would have known that "things happened just as it had been told them." Go and do what the Lord has made known to you and you will discover that things will happen "Just as God has said."

Moving Ahead

*The Lord turned to him and said, Go in
this your might ... Have I not sent you?*
– Judges 6:14 –

Success in your journey is never based on your resources,
it is based on God's sufficiency. God is not looking for the
person with the most natural abilities to accomplish His
will, He is looking for those who are totally dependent
upon Him. He is searching throughout the earth to show
Himself mighty on behalf of those whose hearts are fixed
on Him.

God helps those who can't help themselves. When
God called Gideon to battle, Gideon had nothing
to boast about. He had no confidence in his natural
ability or resources. He was full of fear and His faith
was shaken. Yet God didn't call him a "nobody" but a
"mighty warrior." God told Gideon to step out in his
weakness, and when Gideon did, he found himself walking in God's strength.

Is God calling you to take a new step in the year
ahead, even though you are weak and fearful? When
God calls you, He sends you; when He sends you He
goes with you; when He goes with you, He equips you;
when He equips you, you have everything you need.

In the Coming Year

Lo, I come to do thy will, O God.
– Hebrews 10:9 KJV –

God did not bring you into this world to live without a purpose, to exist without a reason, or function without meaning. You are a unique creation of God. He loves you, cares about you, and wants you to know Him as He knows you.

He has chosen you and prepared you for the work He has called us to do. When your heart is set on His will, you will have the assurance that He will be to you all that you will ever need. This confidence of faith allows you to move through each day with a quiet spirit, inward rest, and joy unspeakable. In the coming year, remember these principles regarding God's will:

1. Place – Be in God's place in His perfect time.
2. Peace – Let His peace keep you at rest.
3. Purpose – Believe God's purpose for you will be fulfilled in the place He has you.
4. Plan – Have confidence that nothing can frustrate God's perfect plan for you.
5. Power – Receive His Spirit to equip and empower you to do what He has called you to do.